Architectural Design
May/June 2008

Interior

**Guest-edited by
Julieanna Preston**

wiley.com

ISBN-978 0470 51254 8
Profile No 193
Vol 78 No 3

Editorial Offices
International House
Ealing Broadway Centre
London W5 5DB

T: +44 (0)20 8326 3800
F: +44 (0)20 8326 3801
E: architecturaldesign@wiley.co.uk

Editor
Helen Castle

Production Editor
Elizabeth Gongde

Project Management
Caroline Ellerby

Design and Prepress
Artmedia Press, London

Printed in Italy by Conti Tipocolor

Advertisement Sales
Faith Pidduck/Wayne Frost
T: +44 (0)1243 770254
E: fpidduck@wiley.co.uk

Editorial Board
Will Alsop, Denise Bratton, Mark Burry, André
Chaszar, Nigel Coates, Peter Cook, Teddy Cruz,
Max Fordham, Massimiliano Fuksas, Edwin
Heathcote, Michael Hensel, Anthony Hunt,
Charles Jencks, Jan Kaplicky, Robert Maxwell,
Jayne Merkel, Michael Rotondi, Leon van Schaik,
Neil Spiller, Michael Weinstock, Ken Yeang

Contributing Editor
Jayne Merkel

Front cover: Foster + Partners, Kamakura House,
Kamakura, Japan, 2004.
© Edmund Sumner/VIEW

Requests to the Publisher should be addressed to:
Permissions Department,
John Wiley & Sons Ltd,
The Atrium
Southern Gate
Chichester,
West Sussex PO19 8SQ
England

F: +44 (0)1243 770620
E: permreq@wiley.co.uk

Subscription Offices UK
John Wiley & Sons Ltd
Journals Administration Department
1 Oldlands Way, Bognor Regis
West Sussex, PO22 9SA
T: +44 (0)1243 843272
F: +44 (0)1243 843232
E: cs-journals@wiley.co.uk

[ISSN: 0003-8504]

AD is published bimonthly and is available to
purchase on both a subscription basis and as
individual volumes at the following prices.

Single Issues
Single issues UK: £22.99
Single issues outside UK: US$45.00
Details of postage and packing charges
available on request.

Annual Subscription Rates 2008
Institutional Rate
Print only or Online only: UK£180/US$335
Combined Print and Online: UK£198/US$369
Personal Rate
Print only: UK£110/US$170
Student Rate
Print only: UK£70/US$110
Prices are for six issues and include postage
and handling charges. Periodicals postage paid
at Jamaica, NY 11431. Air freight and mailing in
the USA by Publications Expediting Services
Inc, 200 Meacham Avenue, Elmont, NY 11003
Individual rate subscriptions must be paid by
personal cheque or credit card. Individual rate
subscriptions may not be resold or used as
library copies.

All prices are subject to change
without notice.

Postmaster
Send address changes to 3 Publications
Expediting Services, 200 Meacham Avenue,
Elmont, NY 11003

C O N T E N T S

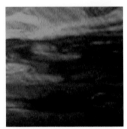

AD+

Joseph William Mallord Turner, *Study for the Sack of a Great House*, c 1830. Oil on
canvas, 908 x 1219 mm; Turner Bequest 1856, Tate Collection, London
This interior scene belongs to a group of paintings of the 1830s that bring the atmospheric
affects associated with Turner's great land and seascapes inside. The figures and interior
details are subsumed by the mist-like air and luminous light.

Editorial

Misty, sculptural, tactile, theatrical and experiential, atmospheric interiors represent a seismic shift for architecture. They celebrate a wholly Romantic sensibility, in which the emotional response overshadows the rational line and the sensory dominates over the intellect. It seems no coincidence that the dictionary definition of the word 'atmosphere' expanded in the late 18th century – the Romantic era in England – from that pertaining solely to planetary gases to the 'sense of surrounding influence, mental or moral environment'.[1] Turner, probably the most renowned Romantic painter, made famous by his stormy seascapes – full of spray and light and air effects – also sought atmosphere in his interiors in the 1830s. When painting the interior of his patron's home, Petworth House in Sussex, he simply brought the mist inside.

Atmosphere brings with it an elusive, but compelling, resonance. So often restaurants, hotels or locations are recommended on the strength of their atmosphere alone. It is this attribute in contemporary life that is able to mark places out from the everyday or the banal – that gives them emotional meaning and human connection. Most often it is historic spaces that are described as atmospheric, evoking with their accumulated traces of human occupation and activity a bygone era, whether a Belle Epoque Parisian brasserie or a medieval manor house.

So what can be in the air of newly completed interiors? Like Turner, guest-editor Julieanna Preston identifies the elusive quality of atmosphere with the metaphor or 'spatial figure' of mist (see p 7), opening the issue with the watery air of Peter Zumthor's Thermal Baths at Vals. She provides us with a multifaceted view of atmosphere in contemporary interiors rather than a single definition. The featured atmospheric spaces are aesthetically diverse, varying from the baroque theatricality of Philippe Starck's restaurant interiors to the restraint of Foster + Partners Kamakura House in Japan pictured on the cover. The emotional engagement that atmosphere evokes in its subject also makes it a potent field for artists and composers as well as architects, interior designers and textile designers, as epitomised by the work of La Monte Young Marian Zazeela in the *Dream House* installation in New York (pp 12–15) and the internal weather affects of Olafur Eliasson (pp 30–5). It is, however, the potential to create spaces that call on all our senses and seduce us with the desire to simply reach out and touch a lumpy wall or a voluminous ceiling that is exhilarating – made reality by the progress of CAD/CAM technologies. It beckons a new era in which the eye has lost some of its ground, and the joy of touch and feeling in a space has gained new value. Δ

Helen Castle

Note
1. www.etymonline.com. Atmosphere: 1638, from Mod.L. *atmosphaera* (1638), from Gk. *atmos* 'vapor' + *spharia* 'sphere'. First used in Eng. in connection with the Moon, which, as it turns out, doesn't have one. Figurative sense of 'surrounding influence, mental or moral environment' is 1797.

In the Mi(d)st Of

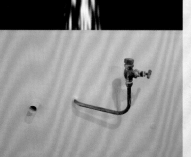

36° Winter   30° Sommer

It's in the air. The first thing that the term atmosphere evokes is in the air, the intangibility of air. A gaseous layer enveloping the planet, a zone where clouds move about, atmosphere is the invisible shroud around each object emanating (such is the meaning that the word has taken on over time) a sort of fragrance or warmth. Atmosphere is created by the particular subject matter or place – it is given off from it – and corresponds to it like a sort of spirit that floats around, revealing, betraying a certain essence of the place or subject matter, but remaining ever visible.

Michel Orsoni, 'Point of view: A question of atmosphere', 1998[1]

Michel Orsoni's words capture the core motivation behind this issue of *AD*; to ferret out where, and how, atmosphere resides. I admit that before guest-editing the issue, I never fathomed just how elusive atmosphere could be. Despite its habit to rove among rational and minimalist architectural shells, stomp brazenly through historic period rooms and infect anaemic gallery and museum institutions, atmosphere evades definition. As the contributions in the issue document, even the most diligent of efforts to unravel atmosphere's impacting constitution highlight its resistance to assume the status of subject. What seems most emphatic is our ability to both recognise and create atmosphere, an ability demonstrated within a wide range of architectural works and creative practices in which atmosphere appears unfettered by its ability to assume multifarious ambient forms or influence spatial perception and experience. Its slippery ephemeral body refuses to be captured, and yet its pervasiveness suggests it is everywhere but nowhere.

The issue adopts mist, a rarefied form of air, as a spatial figure to both contextualise the featured contributions and conceptualise their accumulative effect. As particulate atmosphere-forming matter, mist is a physical phenomenon, a weather pattern dependent on local, intimate and precocious spatial, thermal and temporal factors. Mist, a cloud of water molecules, is site specific and yet geometrically formless. Its visible presence measures a spatial threshold of saturation; water literally falling out of thin air. As an environmental system it signals a weathering mood, perhaps linked to its reference as a political and cultural indicator. As suspended condensation it dramatises a microclimate.

Attesting to a transient constitution, such poetics lend themselves graciously to exploring the atmospheres of interiors as a special kind of mist – one charged by the intensification of enveloping surfaces, the confluence of

---

Far left: **Ying Wang, 'Water Tap' in Filmic Space: Reverie and Matter, 2005**
Ying Wang's digital projection transforms an ordinary interior plumbing fitting into a virtual fountain. Such (mist)ifying design strategies illuminate how atmosphere constructs spatial ambience.

Left: **Peter Zumthor, Thermal Baths, Vals, Switzerland, 1996**
Zumthor's Thermal Baths demonstate a symbolic relationship between hard and soft surfaces, materials and bodies.

multiple inhabiting bodies, the spurious conflation of cultural attitudes towards decoration and ever-changing paradigms of spatiality. In these terms, interiors are understood to be ambient environments delimited by the aura of affect and subjectivity. This issue of *AD* does not attempt to tame mist, but tracks its reformation among a collection of written and visual pieces in an effort to extend our contemporary understanding of how atmosphere, in its tendency to surround, to contextualise and to envelope, resides within the space of interiors. Most importantly, as a rhetorical trope, mist is being used as a trace element of atmosphere, a spatial barium dye that lends visibility to that which is unstable, non-singular and completely relative.

When one attributes an interior with atmospheric qualities, what exactly is being communicated? Does it mean that the room has been designed, stylised or even thematised? Is it a spatial quality that conditions one's experience or perception? What is its subjective element? Does atmosphere originate from material attributes given by interior finishes and decor? Or is it established by the skilful use of lighting and colour to affect drama? Is atmosphere anything like an immersive ambience? How does it coincide with the spatial art of performance whereby event replaces function as a temporal descriptor of inhabitation? How is atmosphere crafted? Such questions establish the theme for the issue, noting that while atmosphere is frequently referenced in design culture, magazines, journals and books, it remains for the most part unexamined.

Two contemporary sources stand out as notable exceptions to the uncharted territory of atmospheres within architectural design: Peter Zumthor's short prosaic book, succinctly titled *Atmospheres* (2006), and the farewell issue of *Daidalos* edited and introduced by Mark Wigley in 1998. In his assertion that atmosphere is an aesthetic category, Zumthor outlines nine ways with which it is crafted as an architectural quality that provokes a spontaneous emotional response, an impression sensed in a fraction of a second. His system of atmospheric factors dwells on material presence coupled with an actual and sensing body to include sound, light, temperature and objects operating within a spatiotemporal context hinged on a tension between proximity of interior and exterior.[2] These aesthetic principles are posited as the ground for Zumthor's built work, a body of architectural practice known internationally for its mastery of crafting material and space.

Also probing its construction, Wigley cites atmosphere's dependence on building and context, crediting it with 'some kind of sensuous emission of sound, light, heat, smell, and moisture; a swirling climate of intangible effects generated by a stationary object'. He aptly reminds us of Semper's argument 'that the full force of architecture is to be found in its outer surface, the decorative layer through which the atmosphere seemingly percolates. Architecture is indistinguishable from décor. To construct architecture is simply to prop up a surface that produces an atmosphere. Architects are special effects experts. The test of their craft is in the thinnest layer of paint, texture or wallpaper.' Wigley subsequently attributes decoration as the outer visible layer of the invisible climate, an envelopment centred on the inhabitant, not the building. In these terms, a building is a device for producing atmospheres, interiors within interiors, demarcated by thresholds of difference. As Wigley calls on Semper's works to direct architectural concerns for atmosphere towards decor, architecture is linked to the craft of illusion. 'The "true atmosphere" of architecture is "the haze of carnival candles". Architecture is but a stage set, never more than theatrical effect.'[3]

What better way to introduce a journal dedicated to interior atmosphere than with a project by Philippe Starck, designer *extraordinaire* of theatrical effects, multisensory experiences and voluptuous objects? Less than a few months after its opening, Le Lan Restaurant, Starck's newest interior environment located on the fourth floor of the LG Twin

Philippe Starck, Le Lan Restaurant, Beijing, China, 2007
A collection of framed mirrors surface the ceiling of this lavishly furnished restaurant and bar.

Signs of eating accoutrements linger on a table surface to attract the entire room towards an imminent feast.

Philippe Starck, Le Lan Restaurant, Beijing, China, 2007
A full compendium of cool- and warm-coloured lighting catches on a
multitude of surface textures from smooth, reflective and slick to hard,
translucent and figured.

strongest design statement towards dematerialising the
product and treating design as an automatic secretion. To
dismiss it as shallow and simple sensory indulgence neglects
the questions and responses it offers about ambience, spatial
effect and technological augmented experience. I note that Le
Lan uses darkness (maybe even blackness) as a spatial
envelope in which to feature illuminated surfaces and objects.
While not a new device for dramatic impact, the ceiling of
framed mirrors expands the depth of that darkness,
multiplies circuitous glimpses from table to table, and repeats
an endless variation of colours and texture. The premise of
this darkness constructs a spatial enclosure, but not a limiting
boundary. Appealing to sensorial pleasure, light-infused
surfaces and objects emanate rather than emit energy.

Le Lan's rich (for some, overly rich) material palette is not
self-conscious or fetishist, but audaciously adventurous. It
establishes a strange frontier of familiar objects restated in a
material language that, according to Starck, are chosen not
for what they are, but for what you can do with them. Le Lan
capitalises on creating an environment well aware of the full
compendium of what Starck calls the sex of an object. The
programme of the restaurant has been exploited as a
sumptuous, maybe even erotic, feast, an expression that is
bound to yield discomfort if one dines to just eat. The energies
generated among feasting bodies, iridescent colour, wafting
curtains and polished reflection are emblematic of our
contemporary zeal for heightened experiences and are,
perhaps, a sign of our resistance to yield to it. Here, Starck
heaves atmosphere out of its decorative trappings into an
intensified field of tactile abundance. Le Lan offers interior
atmosphere as a highly charged event.[5]

Building on a completely different aesthetic and culturally
bounded architectural language, Foster + Partner's Kamakura
House (2004) stimulates an intensified interior mood as a
response to its housing of Buddhist art and the site's historic
and topographic landscape. Featured on the cover of this
issue, it epitomises how interior atmosphere is summoned
through subtle yet innovative material craft: wall panels of
reconstructed stone, backlit glass blocks of recycled cathode-
ray tubes, antique Chinese tiles and glazed volcanic stone tiles
line a concrete structural shell. These material gestures are
greater than their collective material effect. As design team
leader David Nelson states: 'You have to absorb it and let it
slip into your subconscious.'[6]

Several contributions in the issue bear resemblance to the
palpable expressions of interior atmosphere of Le Lan and the
Kamakura House. Ted Krueger's review of La Monte Young
and Marian Zazeela's long-term installation entertains interior
atmosphere produced by sound frequencies to inadvertently
test our reliance on visual ordering devices and representation.
Joel Sanders and Karen Van Lengen present a speculative
design project where the role of sound as a spatial agent as
well as information carrier is shown to permeate conventional
inside–outside boundaries and augment a domestic dwelling
experience. With equal inquisitiveness about relational spatial

Towers in Beijing, already draws comment in design blogs and
popular interior magazines as a place of superlatives, hosting
a Gothic theme, resembling an opium den and exemplifying
'over the top' design decadence. Such reviews reflect more
than the bias that contemporary critics (and many designers)
wage on creative works outside of the Neo-minimalist/Neo-
material sphere of design; they neglect to acknowledge what
motivates the highly saturated environments. Starck's
assertion that the idea of decoration is dead directs
consideration of his work, in particular Le Lan and other
recent restaurants, away from style, especially that of the
eclectic. He states: 'We just now need energy.'[4]

I am struck by the power of Starck's statement in concert
with Le Lan's interior atmosphere. Testing the prevailing
dominance of visual seduction, Le Lan may be Starck's

phenomena, Malte Wagenfeld outlines his study of air and bodily movement, and Hugh Campbell measures the ambient relationship between a photographer's art of visualising and an architect's visualisation of material space.

Olafur Eliasson's conversation with Hélène Frichot knits a discussion between phenomena and perception. Frichot reveals Eliasson's intent to embrace social interaction provoked by large-scale spatial installations that reference cultural conditions beyond the gallery. Rochus Urban Hinkel explores the role of concrete spatial elements in informing subjective spatial perception in a temporary gallery, the Aue Pavilion, taking the form of an industrial greenhouse. Such architecture is shown to foreground the fusion of art and experience, artefact and social event. Lilian Chee discovers how interior atmosphere is regenerated between art installations and the historic context of the Freud Museum. These contributions reveal the manner in which atmosphere projects and reflects a seeing in, seeing through and seeing beyond.

A cluster of contributions form a hinge between the ephemeral face of atmosphere and its material craft. My own contribution challenges digital craft and fabrication designers to extrapolate the affective nature of their design products. Graeme Brooker and Sally Stone visit the office of interior designer Ben Kelly to find that his studio and philosophy mimic his unique use of material: his words and works amend the normative definition of matching or coordinating design aesthetics. Recent interiors by Lewis.Tsurumaki.Lewis (LTL

Architects) position material ingenuity as the principal atmosphere-forming factor. Petra Blaisse reveals to Lois Weinthal how large-scale curtain works cross literal and conceptual inside–outside thresholds serving as programmatic screens and urban cloaks. Working at a similar scale, the newest addition to the IIT campus by Rem Koolhaas envelops an existing rail line as a building patterned by zones of programmatic organisation. Charles Rice locates a new form of atmosphere, the urban interior, in this built work, which transcends conventionalised notions of interior as domestic space.

Rice's contribution introduces another theme lingering within these pages: that of atmosphere's relation to and reliance on specificity of site and place. Just as mist indicates conditions of a microclimate, Mary Anne Beecher argues that Aubrey Watzek's house presents a refined instance where an interior captures a local, regional or vernacular atmosphere. For Paul James, ground is the crucial constituent of one of Walter Pichler's early architectural works: here, we are led between architecture and philosophy to understand atmosphere as a cultural indicator. Rachel Carley identifies a sublime interior atmosphere in the work of Rachel Whiteread, showing how the traces of inhabitation are transported and transformed in the surface of plaster casting, suggesting a ghostly condition of place.

For those interested in underlying ordering tactics, this issue of *AD* consists of three distinct modes of textual discussion, each aimed at culling a diversity of perspectives and types of atmospheric practice within architectural design. Conversant contributions are based on interviews between noted architectural academics and design practitioners, or artists currently engaged in creating some of the most innovative and radical interiors. Evocative contributions take the form of critical reviews reflecting on the interior atmospheres of a fleeing temporal nature – exhibitions, installations, photographic interiors and spatial experiments. Their short-lived nature is shown to rely and confound representation. And lastly, several features fill the role of exploring atmosphere through theoretical speculation. These expanded texts elaborate the finer details of atmosphere's philosophical, cultural and technological temperament.

Julieanna Preston

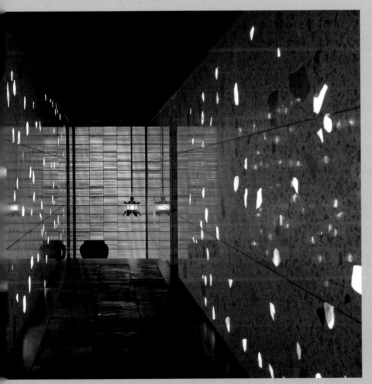

Foster + Partners, Kamakura House, Japan, 2004
The interior atmosphere of the Kamakura House lures one away from clever construction tactics towards the orchestration of their spatial synthesis.

Notes
1. Michel Orsoni, 'Point of view: A question of atmosphere', *Vis A Vis International*, ALA Productions (Paris), 1998, pp 9–11.
2. Peter Zumthor, *Atmospheres: Architectural Environments – Surrounding Objects*, Birkhäuser (Basel), 2006.
3. Mark Wigley (ed), 'The Architecture of Atmosphere', *Constructing Atmospheres*, *Daidalos* No 68, Berlin, 1998, pp 18–27.
4. Philippe Starck Network: www.philippe-starck.com/new/vido/mov6/html (31 December 2007).
5. www.philippe-starck.com (25 November 2007).
6. Michael Webb, 'Distilling Forms in Kamakura: Emphasising Light and Shadow, A Japanese Retreat Updates Tradition', *Architectural Digest*, March 2007.

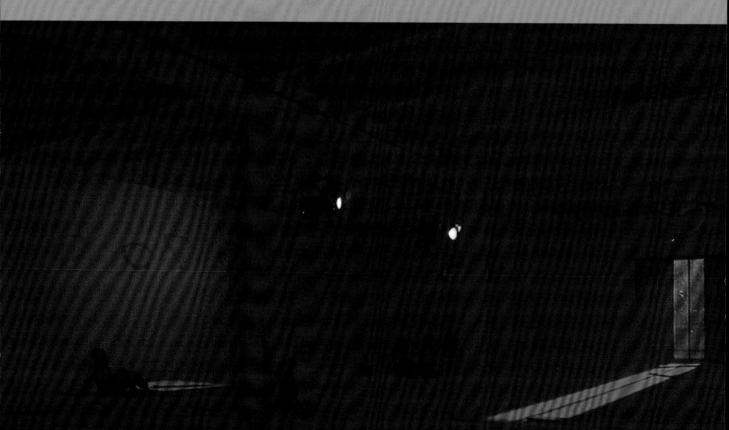

This is Not Entertainment:

Experiencing the *Dream House*[1]

La Monte Young Marian Zazeela, *Dream House: Seven+Eight Years of Sound and Light*, MELA Foundation,
New York, 1993–present; Marian Zazeela, *Imagic Light*, 1993, with *Magenta Day/Magenta Night*, 1993
Light environment installations. White aluminium mobiles, Fresnel lamps, coloured glass filters, electronic
dimmers: Mylar gel mounted on window glass, 3.35 x 7 x 9.75 metres (11x 23 x 32 feet).

Testing the spatiotemporal limits of experience and art installation, *Dream House* dwells upon a physical interaction between bodily movement and synthesised frequencies to prompt a variable sound spectrum and a specific interior atmosphere. Ted Krueger highlights the primacy of first-person experience within a spatial continuum, and in particular an experience of a nonvisual and interactive nature.

Just south of Canal on Church Street in New York's Tribeca district lies an ordinary building housing an extraordinary experience. *Dream House: Seven+Eight Years of Sound and Light* is an installation by composer La Monte Young and artist Marian Zazeela. In a monochromatic room sounds a single chord that has remained unchanged since October 1993. The rich experience obtained within this space directly contrasts this description. The relationship of means-to-ends evident in the work holds insights for architecture and design.

I walk up two long flights of stairs to reach the third level and, after removing my shoes, enter a corridor linking two rooms. The principal room addresses the street; a smaller one lies to the rear. From a formal perspective these spaces are ordinary in every way. Those who seek novelty in shape, space, technology, material or detail will find nothing of interest here. The rooms have no furniture, but several pillows on the floor invite repose. I smell incense. The white walls, ceilings, woodwork and carpet are bathed in an amazing magenta light, and an extraordinary sound pervades the space.

This drone has an ineffable quality; encompassing large portions of the acoustic spectrum including extremely high and low frequencies. As I walk the corridor, the sound shifts subtly. Upon entering the front room, I realise that the frequency and intensity of the tones vary in each ear and that the changes correlate with even the slightest movement. The sound source seems to be, obviously, the huge speakers in each corner, yet this sound cannot be localised in the conventional sense. It does not emanate from somewhere, it simply is. The frequencies are located in space at an extremely fine resolution occupying it in a stable and reliable way. If I

La Monte Young Marian Zazeela, *Dream House 1990: The Prime Time Twins in The Ranges 576 to 448; 288 to
224; 144 to 112; 72 to 56; 36 to 28; with The Range Limits 576, 448, 288, 224, 144, 56 and 28 (1990 VIII 16 c. 1:00
AM NYC) with The Base 9:7:4 (1991–2005)*, Biennale d'Art Contemporain de Lyon, France, 2005
Installation view in a setting of *Primary Light (Red/Blue) x 2* with *Magenta Day/Magenta Night*.

place an ear at a position in three-dimensional space, I will hear a particular tone, and if I return to that location the tone will be heard again. I can cycle through a sequence of frequency combinations by initiating a sequence of movements. By doing so, I can choreograph an acoustic composition. Terry Riley writes: 'Melody is spatially located, since it depends upon where you are sitting or whether you are stationary or moving. As your head moves, your ears behave like fingers on a stringed instrument, activating the various nodes that emphasise different partials of the harmonic spectrum.'[2] By this means, Young has found a way to qualify space, to insert an architecture of sound into an otherwise unoccupied volume.

Since 1984, Young has used a David Rayna-designed interval synthesiser that generates stable phase-locked sine-wave frequencies. When these pure tones sound in an enclosed space with parallel surfaces, the standing waves yield a spatially distributed sound by cancellation or reinforcement. The granularity and richness of this experience is determined by the chosen frequencies and the overall complexity of the chord. Young suggests that there are two distinct ways to listen to this chordal environment: by moving throughout the space and creating melodic sequences, or by sitting quietly listening to a specific set of phase-locked frequencies, by means of which one might attain the 'ultimate experience of "time standing still".[3] When absorbed in this kind of listening, I can detect the movements of another by the sliding shifts in the frequencies that they cause.

I first examine Marian Zazeela's work *Imagic Light* while moving about the main room exploring its acoustic structure. Two white-painted aluminium spirals are suspended along each of the sidewalls illuminated by the red and blue theatre lights that provide the ambient illumination. Two strong and two faint shadows, together with the suspended objects, create a composition that transforms in parallax as I move. Initially this work appears static relative to the changing chord. But this relationship reverses as I stop for an extended period to listen to a set of frequencies. The spirals' ultraslow spin is induced by air currents from a viewer's movements or thermal differences in the room. This creates a slowly changing composition of shadows and objects in varying intensities of contrasting hues. According to Catherine Hennix, this is a dynamic calligraphy with no direct linguistic or symbolic content.[4] Its meaning does not refer to something outside itself, but is given by its phenomenal transformation. Flynt notes that the rare drift into compositional alignment by these dynamically independent objects implies a time scale that can encompass an infinite series of permutations.[5] The group on the north glides momentarily into an approximate bilateral symmetry, and I check the alignment of the group on the other side. Given the scale of the room, the compositions on both sides cannot be compared in a single view, and as I look to the other side I sweep my head through a melody. The interplay between movement and stasis, of sound and light, directly integrates these works. Each becomes the context for the other.

Marian Zazeela, *Ruine Window*, MELA Foundation, New York, 1992, from *Still Light*, 1984–present
Installation view of light sculpture at MELA Foundation *Dream House*. Wood, Fresnel lamps, coloured glass filters, electronic dimmers: 1.54 x 0.6 x 0.2 metres (5.05 x 1.97 x 0.67 feet).

In *Imagic Light*, the projectors illuminate the spirals' continuously varying surface geometry. Depending upon the angle between light, viewer and surface, the spirals take on colour from either or both projectors or magenta backscattered from the environment. Colour might vary continuously across their surfaces, a red luminous line may move along one edge, or the spirals could blend into the background and phenomenally disappear. The slow rotation results in objects that undergo a continuous visual transformation. While the shadows on the wall change shape the fixed geometry that produces them yields a uniform intensity of colour. This luminous shadow is, paradoxically, more present, constant and solid in appearance than the object that produces it. The substance of the shadow and the immateriality of the object is seen again in Zazeela's *Ruine Window* 1992 installed in the smaller room. A composition of white planes parallel or perpendicular to the wall surface is cross-illuminated by red and blue lights. Here again, the shadows achieve an intense colouration, luminosity and presence while the surfaces blend with the background. This phenomenal reversal demonstrates that the relationship between the physical and the perceptual is far more subtle and malleable than is commonly understood.

The sound installation presented in *Dream House* is *The Base 9:7:4 Symmetry in Prime Time When Centered above and below The Lowest Term Primes in The Range 288 to 224 with The Addition of 27 and 261 in Which The Half of The Symmetric Division Mapped above and Including 288 Consists of The Powers of 2 Multiplied by The Primes within The Ranges of 144 to 128, 72 to 64 and 36 to 32 Which Are Symmetrical to Those Primes in Lowest Terms in The Half of The Symmetric Division Mapped below and Including 224 within The Ranges 126 to 112, 63 to 56 and 31.5 to 28 with The Addition of 119.*[6] While a single chord, it is nonetheless one of great complexity. The algorithmic nature of the name suggests tha

La Monte Young Marian Zazeela, *Dream House: The Well-Tuned Piano in The Magenta Lights*, **Kunst im Regenbogenstadl, Polling, Germany; 2001–present**
Long-term installation and DVD projection, with La Monte Young standing in front of his DVD image on the large screen in the *Magenta Day/Magenta Night* environment.

mathematics is the driving organisation and, while important, this is far from the case. The work results from long sessions, in the order of weeks to months, of listening to, of living with, specific sets of tonal intervals. Young writes of an earlier composition: 'After listening to the complex with and without 119 it became clear that the chord was much more beautiful with 119 in it and that it "really belonged".'[7] Note that 119 is again added to the chord presented here. The validation of a particular relationship requires the empirical process of listening over long durations.

Those who choose to engage these works will not find them spare, but extraordinarily rich. This is complexity with clarity rather than the complication of the simple, as is often the rule today. Here, formal originality has been replaced by the primacy of an experience that develops through time. In *Dream House*, I access some small portion of artworks that extend infinitely. The ability to return in order to sample again from this continuum, as I have done on occasion, is central to this notion.[8] It is not surprising that *Dream House* is one in a series of sustained works that Young and Zazeela have undertaken since the 1960s. This body of work develops not only from their artistic practices, but from a manner of living. It evidences a radical understanding of craft and of the effort required to gain a profound knowledge of what one is doing. Both artists have forgone novelty for tightly circumscribed and intensely studied phenomena. Research of this kind rarely occurs in contemporary cultural production. This focus gives the work specific experiential qualities that cannot be yielded by other methods. Work created in this way requires a similar commitment from its audience. It cannot be taken in briefly or casually, nor is it intended to be experienced passively. This is not entertainment. It requires an investment from the participant and rewards them in proportion to their degree of engagement. Its exploration, experience and contemplation may extend for several hours and over many visits. From the visitor's perspective, this is the primary value of an extended installation. ⚙

Notes
1. La Monte Young's programme for a series of concerts given at Yoko Ono's loft in New York City in 1961 contained this notice: 'THE PURPOSE OF THESE CONCERTS IS NOT ENTERTAINMENT.' Cited in Terry Riley, 'La Monte and Marian, 1967', in W Duckworth and R Fleming (eds), Sound and Light, La Monte Young and Marian Zazeela, Bucknell University Press (Lewisburg, PA) and Associated University Presses (London and Cranbury, NJ), 1996.
2. Riley, op cit.
3. La Monte Young, 'The romantic symmetry (over a 60 cycle base) from the symmetries in prime time from 144 to 112 with 119 (89 I 30 NYC)', in Duckworth and Fleming, op cit.
4. Catherine Christer Hennix, 'Language and light in Marian Zazeela's art', in Duckworth and Fleming, op cit.
5. Henry Flynt, 'The lightworks of Marian Zazeela', in Duckworth and Fleming, op cit.
6. The numbers in the title do not refer to frequencies in cycles per second, but to frequency ratios.
7. La Monte Young, op cit.
8. *Dream House: Seven + Eight Years of Sound and Light* is maintained by the Music Eternal Light Art (MELA) Foundation, a not-for-profit arts organisation staffed by volunteers.

Making Sense

The MIX House

In an effort to challenge the dominance of vision over the other senses in architectural experience, **Joel Sanders and Karen Van Lengen** infuse a speculative domestic environment with digital audio technology. Their design capitalises on the augmentation of aural–visual boundaries via technological interventions, ultimately recasting the house from a private and insulated environment to that of a hybridised interactive site.

In our ocular-centric design culture, where does sound fit and how does it inform the development of domestic architecture? The MIX House, a collaborative project between Joel Sanders (JSA), Karen Van Lengen (KVLA) and Ben Rubin (Ear Studio), is a speculative house designed to provoke this enquiry. The project advocates an aural–ocular design strategy, a way of thinking that enlists new technologies to provoke a set of enhanced social and sensory experiences in domestic space.

Since antiquity, western thinkers from Aristotle to Hegel have organised the senses in a hierarchy that validates the age-old opposition between mind and matter, spirit and flesh. Sight, followed by hearing, occupies the top of the sensorial pyramid, with touch, taste and smell, considered to be the 'lower senses', at the bottom. Not unique to philosophy, these prevailing cultural assumptions about the senses have shaped the design of the built environment: western architects have primarily created buildings that appeal to the eye and neglect the body's other senses. But there are exceptional periods in western architectural history that abound with examples of buildings driven by acoustic qualities.

In oral societies, like those of pre-alphabetic Greece and Asia Minor, people prized sonic specificity: cultural exchange and the preservation of collective memory took place in aural space. Consider the perfect clarity of Greek amphitheatres, where a speaker, standing at a focal point created by the precise design of the surrounding walls, is distinctly heard by all the members of the audience. In a similar vein, during the Middle Ages, Romanesque abbeys such as Le Thoronet, and Gothic cathedrals such as Chartres, were valued as much for their acoustic qualities as they were for their visual principles: they functioned as sacred resonators for the recitation of the Christian word.[1] Some critics argue that popular literacy, made possible by the invention of the printed word, triggered a change in this sensate equilibrium, initiating a shift that favoured eye over ear. Although Renaissance architects like Leon Battista Alberti and Andrea Palladio devoted much thought to the intersection of sound, proportion and musical harmony, their work, aided by the newly invented tool of perspective, focused on visual principles, inaugurating the ocular-centric architectural tradition that we have inherited today.

The Modern movement, with its aim of developing a universal 'machine age' aesthetic, further separated a comprehensive relation between space and place. Modern architects such as Le Corbusier and Mies van de Rohe, exploiting the potential of new engineering techniques and materials (concrete, steel and manufactured glass), perfected the curtain wall, allowing them to realise the age-old dream of visual transparency. But while it dissolves the visual borders between inside and outside, the picture window is acoustically silent. Mies' iconic Farnsworth House encapsulates this Modernist tradition. Suspended above the ground plane in a sealed steel-and-glass enclosure, its inhabitants could enjoy uninterrupted panoramic views of the bucolic landscape framed by floor-to-ceiling window walls. These occupants become transfixed spectators, empowered to apprehend the landscape through disembodied vision.

Modern architecture's highly reflective surfaces and largely rectilinear arrangements hosted a range of acoustic problems, commonly known as 'acoustical glare'. In addition, the introduction of environmental control systems, designed for bodily comfort, imposed their own sonic identity that was overlaid on to such interiors. Historian Emily Thompson has argued that these systems, along with the hermetically sealed window walls, effectively cut off our connection to the aural specificity of place.[2]

Mies van der Rohe, Farnsworth House, Plano, Illinois, 1951
With its iconic glass curtain wall, Mies' house exemplifies the authority of visual transparency that dominated the Modern movement.

In the same way that new technologies revolutionised the sensory experience of buildings created by the pioneers of Modern architecture, today one of the most radical but least understood changes in our audiovisual sensory experience of space has been occasioned by the impact of digital technologies. Our sensory experiences are now more than ever affected by audiovisual stimuli transmitted by the proliferation of electronic devices installed in each and every room of our home. Unlike first-generation desktop computers that fixed stationary users in interior space, a new generation of mobile devices – BlackBerries, iPods and iPhones – now allows users to roam freely between inside and outside, public and private space. Some critics lament the introduction of these portable instruments that privatise space, confining individuals to sound bubbles of their own aesthetic choice. Travelling within such solo sound worlds provides people with a false sense of privacy and a deluded sense of control in allowing them to project their personal sonic choices on to the spaces they inhabit. These portable devices not only inhibit people from meaningful social interactions, but also render them indifferent to the sights, sounds and smells of their surroundings.[3]

Joel Sanders, Karen Van Lengen and Ben Rubin, MIX House, suburban neighbourhood in Charlottesville, Virginia, 2006
The kitchen island serves as a new formalised command post, observation centre and nexus of this speculative environment.

Rather than simply repudiate or blindly embrace technological innovation, contemporary architects could evaluate the complex cultural, historical and spatial consequences of their use. Taking the critique of both Modernist acoustics and contemporary mobile technologies to heart, the MIX House project taps into the unrealised potential of new technologies to create opportunities for people to share meaningful audiovisual experiences in space.

MIX House integrates a new kind of window wall within an acoustic design that achieves a condition that we take for granted in media: the integration of sound and image. By incorporating cutting-edge technologies with traditional acoustic principles, the project rethinks and extends the Modernist notion of visual transparency to include aural transparency as well.

Situated on a generic suburban plot, the dwelling is composed of two sound-gathering volumes outfitted with three audiovisual windows. The curved profile of each of these sonic windows operates in one of two ways: when open, a louvred glass window wall admits the sound of the airborne ambient environment, and when closed the window operates as a transparent parabolic dish. The sonic dish includes both a microphone and a small video camera located at its centre that electronically screens and targets domestic sounds and images and transmits them to an interior audio system controlled from the kitchen island.

The living/dining wing, oriented horizontally on the site, frames the driveway at one end and the rear yard at the other, while the den/bedroom wing is oriented vertically to capture audiovisual views of the sky. In the living area, the sonic picture window aimed at the backyard swivels like a camera to extend its range of motion. At the entry, the front window wall doubles as a sliding glass door that allows occupants to hear the sounds of the streetscape.

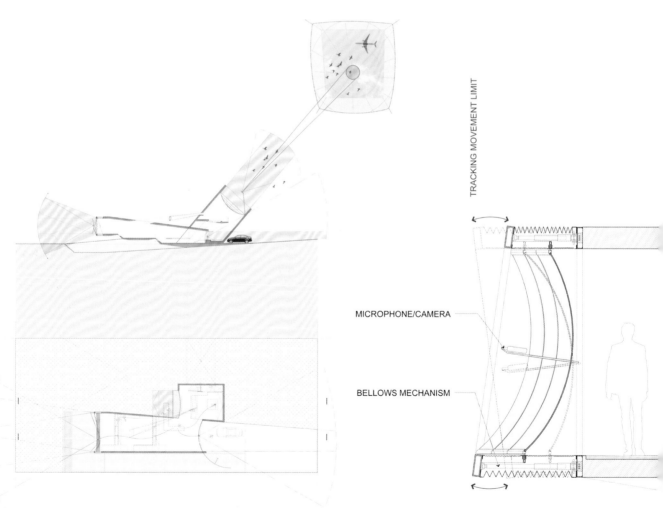

TRACKING MOVEMENT LIMIT

MICROPHONE/CAMERA

BELLOWS MECHANISM

Located on a suburban plot, the MIX House is designed to capture the sights and sounds of the local environment and habitat.

The concave profile of the window wall inset with a microphone and small video captures the sights and sounds of the exterior spaces and transmits them to the Mix Counter in the kitchen.

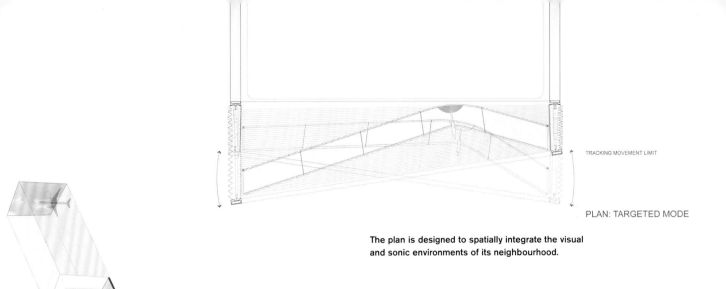

TRACKING MOVEMENT LIMIT

PLAN: TARGETED MODE

The plan is designed to spatially integrate the visual and sonic environments of its neighbourhood.

The section reinforces the planning strategies and rides above the outdoor pool to capture the water images and sounds through window openings located near its centre.

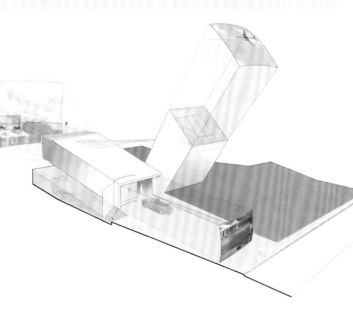

Sectional perspective from the back yard. The MIX House stretches out to its site boundaries to allow inventive interactions in the front yard, the back yard and in the sky.

Audiovisual windows serve practical as well as aesthetic purposes. They allow home owners to filter specific domestic sounds they want to hear or to screen out invasive noises. Sonic windows can also be used to promote creative and collaborative interactions between the house's inhabitants. The communal heart of the house, the kitchen, doubles as a sound command centre, a place where occupants can gather to design impromptu original domestic soundscapes by mixing media-sponsored sounds with the ambient noises of the neighbourhood.

Ultimately, the MIX House offers its occupants the potential to 'know' the domestic environment in an unfamiliar way that calls into question traditional distinctions between nature and culture, music and noise. As John Cage has written: 'Wherever we are ... what we hear is mostly noise. When we ignore it, it disturbs us ... When we listen to it, we find it fascinating.'[4] ⅅ

Notes
1. Ted Sheridan and Karen Van Lengen provide a useful overview of how traditional architecture was generated according to sonic principles in 'Hearing architecture, exploring and designing the aural environment', *Journal of Architectural Education*, Vol 57, November 2003, pp 37–44.
2. Emily Thompson, *The Soundscape of Modernity: Architectural Acoustics and the Culture of Listening in America 1900–1933*, MIT Press (Cambridge, MA), 2002.
3. Michael Bull, 'Auditory', in Caroline A Jones (ed), *Sensorium*, MIT Press (Cambridge, MA), 2006, pp 112–14.
4. John Cage, 'The future of music: Credo', in Dan Lander and Micah Lexier (eds), *Sound by Artists*, Art Metropole and Walter Phillips Gallery (Toronto), 1990, p 15.

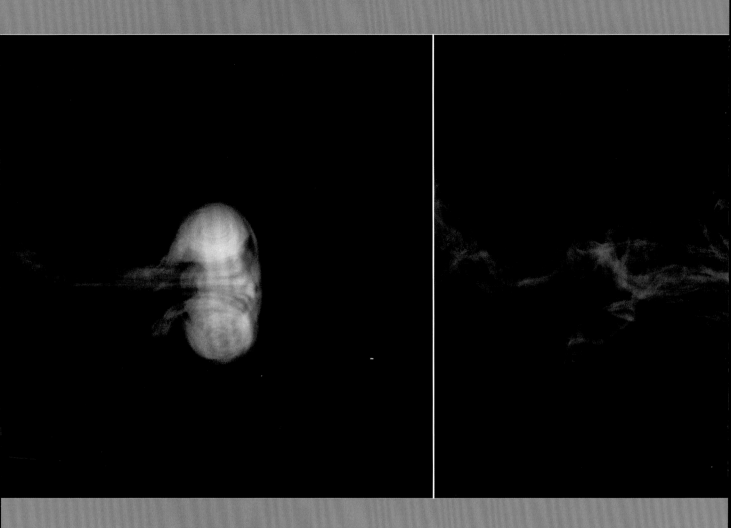

The Aesthetics of Air

Malte Wagenfeld tackles the difficult problem of visualising air, and in his physical experiments reveals a world of eddies, swirls and wafting particles circulating around moving bodies. Here he offers a literal and conceptual glimpse at the invisible nature of atmosphere.

The aesthetic and sensual qualities of air are unusual terrain for an industrial designer. While exploring the formal and kinetic possibilities of unconventional fan blade geometries, I observed that a number of blades generated irregular patterns of air movement. Initially I saw these irregularities as a problem, but when I considered the perceptual effect, I realised it approximated natural 'outside' air. This discovery turned my curiosity from the physical object to the sensual perception of air movement and how this could be

manipulated as a design medium, setting the stage for an incredibly rich experiment. At first the investigation focused on simulating the type and variety of air-based experiences encountered in an outside environment, but this quickly broadened to encompass the overall aesthetic perception of air within interior spaces and its associated qualities linked to smell, humidity, density, sound and so on.

I was dealing with something that was both formless and invisible. How does a designer trained in manipulating form largely for visual effect approach such an intangible medium? My instinct was to appropriate high-end computing and fluid visualisation software as a design tool. But this distancing from the medium seemed to be in opposition to the very idea of the investigation. The sensorial perception of air is a dynamic physiological experience that calls for a corporeal exploration with the body as a perceptual instrument at its centre. The uncharted design territory of exploring air phenomena meant that the first stages of the investigation

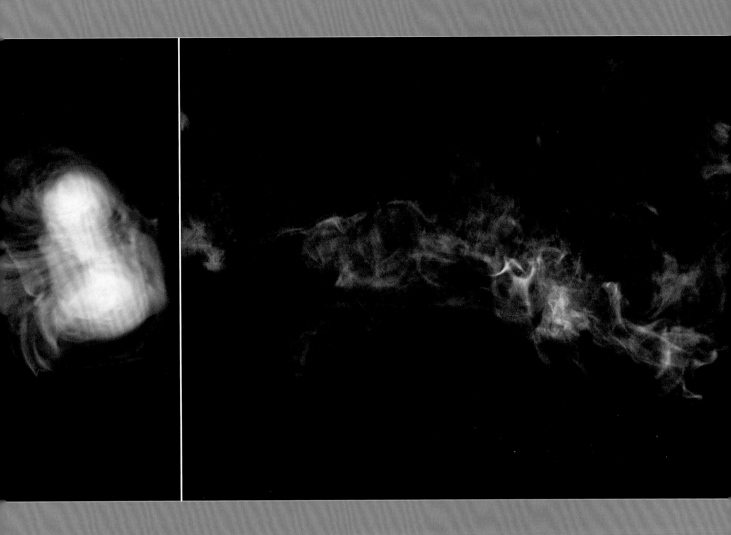

Experiments in Visualising the Invisible

required focusing on observing and manipulating phenomena rather than devising mechanisms that generate phenomena. The investigation thus became a phenomenological study.

Initial investigations focused on observing outside air movement as evidenced by fluttering leaves, swaying branches and grass, the rippled surface of water and so on. Careful analysis using video documentation indicated that air movement was not only random, but also highly localised. I observed that while leaves on one branch of a tree were fluttering, those only metres away were completely still. In a single moment this relationship shifted. This was an important observation because although I had previously

considered outside air to be random, I had not thought it to consist of such highly localised phenomena. The process of looking highlighted that the perceptual nuances of outside air movement are both spatial and temporal.

Observation of subtle air movements experienced in interior spaces required a more sophisticated method of visualisation. The ability for light to reveal dust particles or smoke floating in the air was the inspiration behind the technique of visually rendering air movement. A laser and spinning mirror were used to produce a wafer-thin sheet of light into which smoke was introduced, producing a planar dissection of air. The experiments were conducted in a

Malte Wagenfeld and Ian de Gruchy, Experiments in generating air phenomena, 2007
As part of the 'visualisation of air' investigation, I began exploring the generation of air phenomena. This vortex, generated by an apparatus constructed in my studio, is a self-propelling body of air slowly moving through an interior space. As a consequence of this experiment, I began to observe air phenomena rather then generating them.

Malte Wagenfeld, PF Type 1, 1999
A 1.6-metre (5.25-foot) tall vertical axis
pedestal fan with flexible closed cell foam
blades. Part of an exploration into
unconventional fan blade geometries exploring
kinetic and formal possibilities, this fan
generates a highly irregular pattern of air
movement approximating that of 'outside' air.

The initial intent of the planar dissection of air was to visualise and map major air currents within a naturally ventilated interior
environment. A CAD model of the Melbourne warehouse was constructed to assist in planning for these experiments. This image
shows a series of proposed dissections through the vertical north–south plane and the horizontal plane.

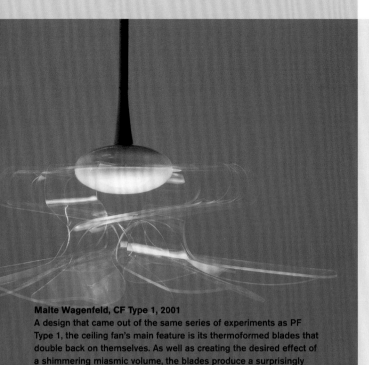

Malte Wagenfeld, CF Type 1, 2001
A design that came out of the same series of experiments as PF
Type 1, the ceiling fan's main feature is its thermoformed blades that
double back on themselves. As well as creating the desired effect of
a shimmering miasmic volume, the blades produce a surprisingly
'natural' randomised pulsating movement of air.

**Malte Wagenfeld, Jason Parmington, Ramesh Ayyar and
Ian de Gruchy, The planar dissection of air, 2007**
Smoke as it is first introduced from the 'fogger' into the
wafer-thin sheet of laser light.

Once the smoke has settled, the highly complex patterns of air movement
are revealed. Shown is a plane approximately 3 x 3 metres (9.8 x 9.8 feet).

converted warehouse in Melbourne chosen for its interior
space, light and character. The generous yet still intimate
volume of the interior and the sightly porous old louvred
factory windows combined to generate a gentle, barely
perceptible yet continuous movement of air. A small team was
assembled to operate the apparatus and aid in performing
various parts of the investigation.

The experiments were devised to map air currents within
the interior space. Like the diagrams of blue and red arrows
drawn by engineers and architects, I expected the air to behave
and circulate in a discernible manner. For example, stronger air
velocity was expected near the windows and floor, and less in
the centre of the room or near the ceiling. However, it soon
became apparent how simplistic this premise was.

Our first impression was of pure amazement. The air was
revealed to us as a highly complex set of paisley-like patterns
of gently spinning vortices that had the delicacy of fine lace. It
was as though we had been granted another sense. A
spectacular hidden world was made known to us. The air
within the space seemed to be moving in no particular
direction; but all directions at once. Swirling bodies of air
were seen moving north–south, east–west, up–down and
crossways, sometimes slicing past each other like people in a
crowd, sometimes spiralling into one another and then
moving off together on a new trajectory. Now and again,
larger nebulae of air, about the size of apples, would slowly
rotate on their axis, moving leisurely through the space at
about a centimetre a second. These fine patterns of air were
clearly part of a larger system of highly complex relationships
created by a multiplicity of currents and interactions.

With the objective of understanding how occupation
affected air within a space, we began experimenting with
simple acts of habitation. A breath gently exhaled in parallel
with the laser light could be observed travelling over 6 metres
(19.7 feet) across a room tracing a flowing trail through the
patterns. The waving of a traditional Japanese fan would gently
shuffle the swirling vortices and hasten their movement. The
opening of a door, even though it was 5 metres (16.4 feet) away,
registered almost immediately as a flurry of activity.

Most surprising of all was how the motion of our bodies
impacted on the air. A person approaching the laser light
would part the smoke-filled air, creating a door-like opening.
Having passed through the light, a slightly enlarged imprint
of his or her body was momentarily visible before the air,
apparently clinging to the individual's body, spiralled behind
him or her, closing this virtual door; an effect reminiscent of
Orpheus entering the underworld though a mirror in Jean
Cocteau's film *Orphée*.

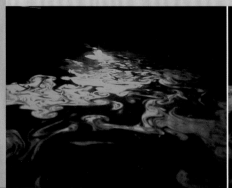
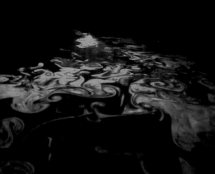
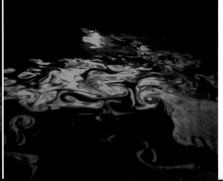

Malte Wagenfeld, Jason Parmington, Ramesh Ayyar, Ian de Gruchy and Polly Watkins,
Experiments with acts of habitation: breathing into the planar dissection, 2007
A person's breath is visually revealed as a major gesture as it moves across the room.

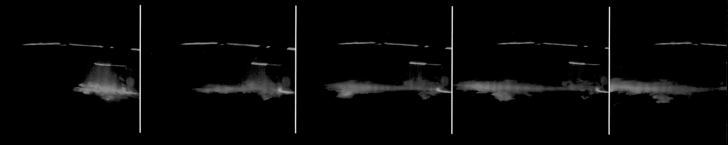

Repeating the experiment several times with different subjects demonstrated that the pattern of air movement generated
by a breath has its own identifiable visual language; a central shaft flanked by two smaller eddies on either side.

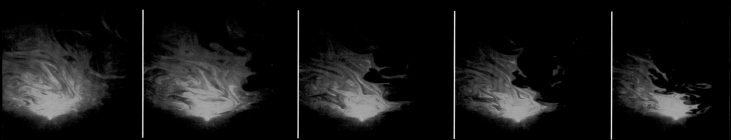

Malte Wagenfeld, Jason Parmington, Ramesh Ayyar and Ian de Gruchy, Experiments with acts of habitation: opening a door, 2007
This sequence of five images shows how the opening of a door produces a dramatic displacement of air within the interior environment.

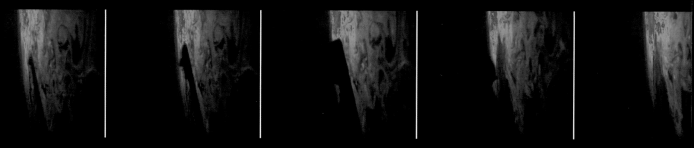

Malte Wagenfeld, Jason Parmington, Ramesh Ayyar, Ian de Gruchy and Polly Watkins, Experiments with acts of habitation: walking into the dissection, 2
As a person passes through the laser dissection of air, a shadowy imprint remains momentarily visible leaving temporal evidence of bodily presence.

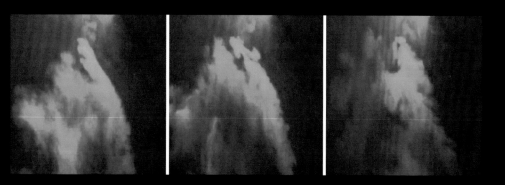

Malte Wagenfeld, Jason Parmington, Ramesh Ayyar and Ian de Gruchy, Experiments with acts of habitation: electric fans, 2007
When a desk fan was turned on 7 metres (23 feet) from the laser dissection, the gentle patterns of air were immediately destroyed
and replaced by a billowing mass resembling a cumulus cloud.

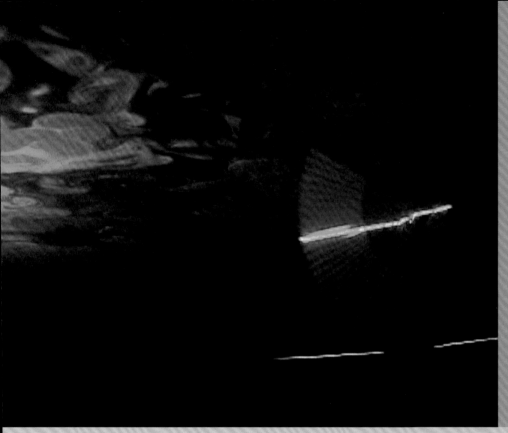

Malte Wagenfeld, Jason Parmington,
Ramesh Ayyar and Ian de Gruchy,
Experiments with acts of habitation: waving
of a traditional Japanese fan, 2007
When the fan was waved gently the patterns
of air appeared to be shuffled, while a more
vigorous movement began to diffuse and
mix the air.

However, when we turned on a desk fan 7 metres (23 feet) from the laser dissection the intricate and delicate patterns of air were destroyed in an instant, and replaced by a billowing body of smoke, demonstrating not only how complex this system of air is, but also how fragile. The system of air had seemingly switched from a highly random but visually coherent state to an incoherent chaotic state. Not only does the air movement created by an electric fan feel different, it also creates a strikingly different visual effect.

The experiments confirmed that air in a voluminous, naturally ventilated space is constantly moving. The extent, complexity, intricacy and multidirectional nature of this movement was utterly unexpected. The swirling currents of air appear to randomly stimulate the body from all angles concurrently. This behaviour, in part, may explain why air in a cathedral feels so different from air in a small room. Perhaps most unexpected was how occupants and their actions within a space become contributors to the prevailing system of air movement; the occupant impacts on the air and the air impacts on the occupant.

In the context of the larger design investigation, three important insights come to the fore. First, that the air within an interior space is highly randomised; second, that dynamic relationships exist between our bodies, space and air; and third, that the system of air movement is fragile, susceptible to even the slightest of external factors. Significantly, 'seeing' air has heightened all my senses.

As a consequence I have begun to visualise and imagine interior spaces quite differently. Consider a space such as the domed reading room in the State Library of Victoria.[1] The qualities of the interior with its associations of knowledge and contemplation impart a very particular atmosphere. The air within the library's massive stone walls is voluminous, cool, lofty and relatively constant. It also has a very particular odour; the odour that a large volume of old books secretes. These are qualities that do not change on a daily basis. However, the air also has very definite temporal qualities, seasonal variations and slight fluctuations from day to day, and then at a micro level it is constantly changing, maybe an outside breeze entering an air vent, a door opening, a person rushing past, a large book being closed. These actions leave temporal traces of air movement. The experiments in visualising air rendered these subtle traces as grand gestures revealing the unexpected spatial relationship between ourselves, our actions and the air we inhabit.

As a result I no longer just feel or imagine such subtle traces: I now have the beginnings of a visual grammar with which to envisage air in four-dimensional temporal space, as well as the building blocks for a vocabulary with which to describe such phenomena. Making associations between images and words allows me to describe, for example, a slowly moving luminous disc of air as a nebula. This vocabulary can now be developed to encompass the many other perceptual qualities of air such as scent, temperature, density, humidity, sound; the air and all that which is carried by it. ∆

Note
1. Originally built in 1854 from massive Victorian bluestone blocks lined with Tasmanian sandstone, the library's main architectural feature is the 1913 addition of the enormous domed reading room which measures 34.74 metres (114 feet) in diameter and height, and houses the library's rare and extensive Australiana collection.

Domestic Afterlives

Rachel Whiteread's *Ghost*

The original room at 486 Archway Road in Islington, north London. The artist corrected undercuts and rectified uneven floor levels within the room prior to casting it. A casting pattern was then devised around the room's defining architectural features including the fireplace, window, door and picture rail.

Long associated with uncanny atmosphere, ghosts suggest a lingering presence of something past. **Rachel Carley's** examination of Rachel Whiteread's *Ghost* belies the role that the plaster-casting process makes towards visualising the invisible. In turn, the vestigial traces of a room's surface are refigured as a solid volume capable of depleting light and heat from the space of the museum.

In 1988, Rachel Whiteread had her first solo exhibition at the Carlisle Gallery in Islington, London. The exhibition consisted of a collection of plaster casts derived from pieces of postwar furniture. After making these furniture castings, the artist turned her attention to the larger issue of the room. The wall of the space became the subject rather than the room's contents. *Ghost* (1990) is a plaster cast taken in sections from the walls of a small room in a derelict Victorian terraced house in north London. The artist wrote her own brief for *Ghost*, with the aim of 'mummifying the air in the room and making it solid'.[1] Whiteread employed her signature reworking of the lost-form casting process to spatially and materially transform the interior. During the casting process the mould is usually destroyed when the cast is created. Whiteread thwarts this process by exhibiting the mould, which is a negative of the original object. *Ghost* foregrounds the inward-looking, opaque qualities of Victorian domestic space in contrast to Modernist space conceptions of the interior that aimed to dissolve the boundaries between inside and outside.

Within the catalogue of ghost species this sculpture can be likened to the 'fetch', the ghost of someone living who is about to die. *Ghost* was carefully and deliberately conjured from the ether blanketing the interior limits of the room, manifesting an afterlife for an abandoned piece of architecture.[2] Thus *Ghost*

Rachel Whiteread, *Ghost*, 1990: plaster on steel frame, 270 x 318 x 365 cm, private collection
Ghost sculpture installed in the Van Abbemuseum, Eindhoven, Germany, in 1993. Under Whiteread's direction, the hearth is rendered inoperable. It is relieved of its literal and metaphorical burdens to provide thermal comfort and also function as the very centre of the 19th-century home.

Whiteread's casting practice transformed the room's architectural profiles and drew attention to elements such as the doorknob and keyhole: details whose psychic impact on the subject far outweighs their physical size.

operates as a spectral entity by obfuscating the distinctions between visible and invisible realms in architecture. *Ghost* is a double not brought to full sculptural term, a double subject to completion as the artist withholds the reproductive imperative traditionally allied to casting practices.

Whiteread's transformation of the room evokes a haunting atmosphere on many levels. Haunting can be both extramundane and mundane; it can be mobile or site specific. To haunt is to be insistently and disturbingly present, particularly in someone's mind. A haunt is also a location frequented often. To be haunted is to bring past impressions to bear on current circumstances, interpreting new phenomena in light of them. *Ghost* bears the impressions of the specific room from which it was cast, but it is also laden with the impressions of past rooms brought to bear on it by viewers.

To achieve this haunting atmosphere, Whiteread robs the interior of heat and light: it becomes a desiccated adumbration of its former self. The work is apprehended in a manner that can be likened to an out-of-body experience, as the viewer observes the cast of the room from the perspective of the room itself.

A ghost usually returns to haunt the terrestrial scene of its death. However, in this instance the ghost and the scene itself were coincident, separated only by a liminal skin of release agent. The sculpture disallows access to the interior in any

legible form: we are evacuated from the interior space the room once harboured and dissociated from the site to which it refers. Indeed, it was not until Whiteread assembled *Ghost* in her studio for the first time that she realised what she had made. When she saw the negative impression of the light switch she realised she had created a space from which she was completely shut out. Her viewer position was now coincidental with that of the wall.

Displaced from the site that shaped its profile and now haunts it, *Ghost* returns to haunt the various institutions in which it finds itself. The atmosphere it generates alters dramatically in relation to the size and scale of the space in which the sculpture is exhibited. When it was placed in the capacious Saatchi Gallery at the Boundary Road site in Camden (1992), *Ghost's* footprint appeared especially meagre, drawing attention to the smallness of the spaces in which many of us live out our existence. In comparison, when shown in the low-ceilinged Chisenhale Gallery in Bethnal Green (1990), the work dominated the space, affording the sculpture a monumental aspect belied by the original room's humble provenance.

This phantasmic construction signals manifold returns of the repressed that render it an emblem of the uncanny. Anthony Vidler notes that Ernst Jentsch attributed a feeling of

Ghost sculpture installed in the Chisenhale Gallery, London (1990). *Ghost* is perceived from the perspective of the room itself, blocking up each of its interior corners. The viewer can now only evaluate the interior of the room as a series of elevations, one wall at a time.

uncanniness to 'a fundamental insecurity brought about by a "lack of orientation", a sense of something new, foreign and hostile invading an old, familiar, customary world.'[3] *Ghost's* method of construction and exhibition serve to disturb and unsettle the subject's relation to interior space. Its wall surfaces were divided into plaster sections, rendering visible a grid of construction lines manifested as breaches in *Ghost's* material constitution. Whiteread wanted viewers to look between the gaps in the plaster sections of the cast to get a glimpse of the innermost interior, exposing the rough-hewn underside of the sculpture. The desire to covertly access the interior had its origin in a fascination with looking between the cracks into the post-mortem residencies in Highgate Cemetery in London where the artist once worked.[4] The 'unnaturalness' of the room's representation is also exacerbated by the sculpture's material verisimilitude, serving to subsume all architectural details found within the room into a homogenising mould.

Ghost reveals hidden or overlooked aspects of the domestic interior, bringing them to light. Whiteread's casting technique was utilised to represent a building typology that modern architects sought to repress: the 19th-century domicile. Domestic architecture of this period stood accused of inducing pathological neuroses. Vidler has observed that the free plan of the Modernist dwelling was promoted as an

Ghost sculpture installed in the Saatchi Gallery, Boundary Road, London (1992). The proportions of the plaster sections of the interior walls were prescribed by what could be taken out of a door and down a domestic staircase.

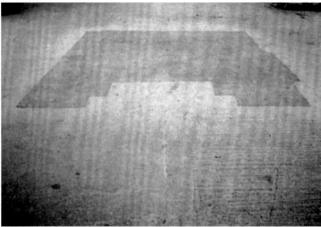

The underside of *Ghost*. On completion of casting, the plaster sections of the room were reassembled off site and hung from an internal steel armature.

Rachel Whiteread, *Ghost of Ghost*, photograph of floor plan of the *Ghost* sculpture in dust, 1990
Ghost is an emblem of the architectural uncanny as it effaces the distinction between imagination and reality, replacing the derelict room with a spectre of its former self.

antidote to 19th-century housing forms, which were believed to have harboured domestic secrets and promoted antisocial behaviour.[5] Under Whiteread's mandate this 19th-century domestic interior comes back to haunt Postmodern space. Space, the material employed by modern architects to dissolve the divisions between inside and outside, has been coagulated. By employing plaster as her casting medium, the artist also recovers the particular maculations left on the interior over time, such as the ash deposits embedded on the fire grate and traces of yellowing wallpaper stained by nicotine. The sculpture foregrounds evidence of weathering that Modern architecture sought to repress. Moshen Mostafavi and David Leatherbarrow have noted that stains, an omnipresent threat to whitewash, were categorised by Modern architects as deformities to be eliminated. They were seen as 'faults, to be suppressed both technically and morally'.[6]

The space the viewer occupies in relation to *Ghost*, the space between the gallery walls and the plaster shell, the room as representation, is a space inscribed by loss and desire. There is the loss of the room as a spatial enclosure and a desire to recuperate or comprehend this room by attempting to reconfigure the original object from the negative cast, or by peering between the cracks. This sense of loss is iterated by the title Whiteread bestows upon the work: the ghost is a leitmotif of loss and desire, a spectral figuration of the lost object desired by the subject in mourning.

Recent technological innovations have inaugurated new forms of disembodied communication. The Internet is our pre-eminent modern-day medium, enabling us to instantly access distant places and people, actual or imagined, living or long gone. Within the digital design realm, contingent, ephemeral effects can be deployed to generate spectral atmospheres on demand. Diaphanous apparitions can free-float within cyberspace, shifting axes at will. Whereas modern media such as television and the Internet offer instant spectral

gratification by conserving images that return to repeatedly haunt us, *Ghost* slows this transmutation down. The sculpture initiates an exchange between insides and outsides, past and present, and irrupts chronology. *Ghost* takes time to look at and distil. The sense of disorientation it evokes is coupled with a complex sense of duration. *Ghost* exhibits two temporal indexes simultaneously: the impressions of age gleaned directly from the room in conjunction with those of the plaster cast itself.

Ghost provides evidence of a domestic afterlife. The spirit of a dead interior is made manifest, as the artist reconfigures and reinvigorates the significance of a demoted, quotidian space, rendering our relationships to our habitual haunts deeply ambivalent. This extrovert interior is disquieting because it destabilises our relation to the domestic space. Whiteread's work petitions architects to look in detail at quotidian environments, to acknowledge and take account of what the occupier brings to the interior: their marks of habitation, their decorative predilections and favoured furnishings, which substantially affect how the architecture is occupied, and how atmosphere is constructed. ⌂

Notes
1. Beryl Wright, 'Option 46: Rachel Whiteread', in *Options*, Museum of Contemporary Art (Chicago), 1993, p 3.
2. Prior to casting the room, undercuts needed to be corrected and uneven floor levels rectified. A casting pattern was then devised around the room's defining architectural features. The cast plaster sections of the room were then reassembled off site and hung from an internal steel armature.
3. Anthony Vidler, *The Architectural Uncanny: Essays in the Modern Unhomely*, MIT Press (Cambridge, MA), 1992, p 23.
4. Jan Debbaut and Selma Klein Essink (eds), *Rachel Whiteread*, Stedelijk Van Abbemuseum (Eindhoven), 1992–3, p 10.
5. Anthony Vidler, 'A Dark Space', in James Lingwood (ed), *Rachel Whiteread: House*, Phaidon (London), 1995, p 67.
6. Moshen Mostafavi and David Leatherbarrow, *On Weathering: The Life of Buildings in Time*, MIT Press (Cambridge, MA), 1993, p 88.

Olafur Eliasson
and the Circulation of
Affects and Percepts

In Conversation

Hélène Frichot's conversation with Olafur Eliasson reveals the depths to which his work mobilises atmosphere as an agent of human experience and social action, prompting a subjective transformation. Light and colour play significant parts in culling affective atmospheres open to multiple perceptions focused on the ephemeral.

Olafur Eliasson, *Notion motion*, Museum Boijmans van Beuningen, Rotterdam, The Netherlands, 2005
An interior wall dissolves vertiginously into ripples of light.

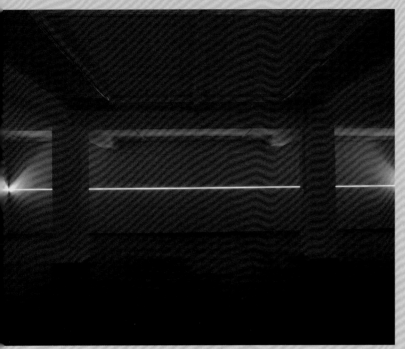

Olafur Eliasson, *Your activity horizon*, Reykjavik Art Museum, Iceland, 2004
A line of brilliant light shifts across a spectrum of colours creating an altered horizon of perception.

The work of Danish-Icelandic artist Olafur Eliasson is suffused with an internal atmosphere that profoundly impacts upon all those who experience it. Eliasson creates framed interior spaces that improbably reproduce an array of manufactured weather conditions and wild and moody landscapes. These atmospheric installations prove particularly compelling for interior and architectural designers, as affects and percepts are combined to constantly circulate and create an intimate relay between the artwork and those who enter into contact with it. Through the manipulation of colour, transparency and the reflection of light, Eliasson dissolves the material of interior space into the immaterial sensory quality of atmosphere and captures the receptive visitor in this embrace. A tentative theory of affect will be explored here in order to discover how Eliasson undertakes the mutual transformation of space, time and habitation.

The immaterial materials of atmosphere that Eliasson manipulates move beyond mere surface effect, opening up new formations of the social. This article draws on 'Life in Space', a midsummer forum held in June 2007 at Studio Olafur Eliasson, located in a former freight warehouse, which is adjacent to the Hamburger Bahnhof, Museum für Gegewart, a contemporary art museum in Berlin. The reoccurring themes of the longest day of the year included temporality, or the inexorable sensation of the passing of time; the status of reality; the primacy of the object, specifically in relation to the position of the art object in contemporary art, and the medium of the model and maquette; and the perception of colour and light, as exemplified by the phenomenon of photographic reproduction. These themes erupted as a collective conversation that developed openly among all the invited participants.

During the midsummer gathering, questions persistently arose around the subject of responsibility and ethics, and the contribution of art to new forms of sociability and community. The atmospheric pressure of Eliasson's work is such that it demands the visitor's engagement beyond that of a mere onlooker; it is an interaction that encourages the mutual transformation of both the visitor and the artwork. Most accounts of Eliasson's *The weather project*, housed in the Turbine Hall of Tate Modern (16 October 2003 to 21 March 2004), describe how visitors were sprawled across the ground, transfixed by the looming interior sun and the subtle shifts in light and humidity, as well as their own images reflected back to them from the mirrored ceiling high above. In discussing atmosphere, which has such a strong position in the artist's own vocabulary, a surprising but important link can be made

Olafur Eliasson, *The weather project*, Unilever Series, Turbine Hall, Tate Modern, London, 2003
Spectators are transfixed in the immense volume of the Turbine Hall, which transformed into an interior landscape watched over by a warm sun and intermittent swathes of mist.

Olafur Eliasson, *Your mobile expectations: BMW H₂R project*, 2007
The new body of the BMW hydrogen-powered car is composed of two curved layers of intricately laced, reflective metal shards, which are augmented by a third layer composed entirely of ice.

with new models of social interaction. Eliasson's aspiration is that his studio should operate as an experimental laboratory open to outside influences and collaboration rather than as a 'closed cell'. Hence the importance of the symposium's location in his studio; the second of its kind, this invited symposium was supported by Eliasson's collaboration with the BMW Art Car programme.

The projects discussed in the greatest detail included Eliasson's transformation of the BMW H₂R hydrogen-powered car, entitled *Your mobile expectations: BMW H₂R project* (2007), as well as the Serpentine Pavilion, London (2007), which Eliasson collaborated on with the Snøhetta architect Kjetil Thorsen. The symposium experiment was curated to capture a microcosm of reality, and as Eliasson explained at its inception: 'I want to create this kind of coming together.' It

became more apparent as the day progressed that for Eliasson atmosphere is inextricably linked with social encounter.

Light is one of the fundamental materials – albeit substance-less – that Eliasson manipulates across his *oeuvre*, from the *Notion motion* (2005) installation, where walls are rendered seemingly immaterial by way of effects of light, through to the horizon series, for example *Your activity horizon* (2004) and *Your black horizon* (2005), where space is split apart by the brilliant line of an artificial horizon. The second-person pronoun of the titles clearly places the ownership of the artwork with the beholder: the art is incomplete without the uncertainty of the one who perceives it.

After lunch on the day of the symposium, Eliasson asked the participants to quietly gather round and focus their attention unflinchingly on a wall of the studio. A studio

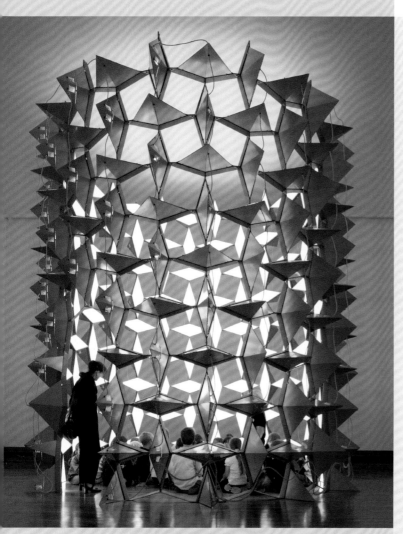

Olafur Eliasson, *The inverted shadow tower*, 2004
An interior pavilion flooded with light shelters a cluster of children.

Affect is the movement between emotional registers rather than the emotion itself once it can be named. Likewise, the percept is less about the named perception than what happens in the encounter that causes a pure percept to emerge. The percept facilitates a landscape of sensation to unfurl. Eliasson's interior landscapes produce a powerful impact as they make visible the erstwhile imperceptible force of a world. Even when he is manipulating the surface of an object such as the BMW H_2R hydrogen-powered car, the manner in which such objects are enclosed in their own environments is crucial. All that appears to remain of the BMW H_2R car that was delivered to Eliasson's studio in 2005 are the wheels, the interior frame of the driver's seat and the steering wheel. A filigree of reflective metal shards is laced in two layers to form a permeable carapace that replaces the original body of the car. The entire construction is kept in a controlled environment maintained at subzero temperatures. The surface of the car accretes a cloak of ice, including the formation of precarious icicles, and the augmented car is lit from within by an apocalyptic yellow glow. Operating as an omen of a future turned sour through environmental disaster, the project is intended to temporally relocate the visitor in an anticipated ice age. We become visitors from the past exposed to the future implications of our consumptive habits.

Eliasson's work also includes a series of pavilions, or follies, among which can be counted *The inverted shadow tower* (2004), *La situazione antispettiva (The antiperspective chamber)* (2003) and, most recently, his collaboration with Kjetil Thorsen of Snøhetta for the 2007 Serpentine Gallery Pavilion, London. In relation to his work on the Serpentine Pavilion, Eliasson explains that he is especially interested in the role of the model, not as a representative and lesser version of a reality yet to be realised, but as a reality in its own right. He argues that in addition to objects such as houses and artworks, 'we also find models of engagement, models of perception and reflection'. As models are steeped in political and individual intent, they contribute to new kinds of social relations that allow us to understand that 'what we have in common is that we are different'. To support this argument, the 2007 Serpentine Pavilion is not just a foray into the medium of architecture, but opens up a forum for a series of experimental events. Eliasson's work is optimistic in its provocation that together we can explore how future forms of community can be ventured through the distribution of the sensible, or else the way sensations are aroused through design and art practice and how these sensations impact on our shared as well as distinct social practices. Forms of community are not so much united under some common sense; instead they can share their differences through an experience of multifarious sensations.

If it can be said that we suffer a contemporary waning of affect in our contemporary world of empty consumerism, then it is only through art such as Eliasson's, with its atmospheric augmentations, that we return to a realm of affect and percept. This increases our capacity for existing well in a

assistant arranged for a projection to be cast on to the wall, which displayed a circling ring of blue dots. By increments it appeared that the blue dots transformed into orange smudges. Our optical apparatus completed the story, providing the orange afterglow, which is a mere perceptual illusion created by the passage of blue. Each spectator participated in the work not as a passive receiver of information, but as an active subjectivity contributing to the production of the percepts and affects of the event. Eliasson explained that each one of us is crucial to the completion of the story of light that unfolds. If each participant experiences a slightly different affect, it is through the negotiation of his or her perceptual disagreement that he or she manages to form a community of sorts.

In this context, affects must be understood not as mere emotions: I feel happy, I feel sad. Instead, affects are the transformative shifts in register that allow the subject to recognise his or her subjectivity in transformation or, as Eliasson puts it: 'We learn to see ourselves in a different light.'

Olafur Eliasson, Serpentine Gallery Pavilion, London, 2007
Set in Kensington Gardens, the pavilion spirals up to the level of the surrounding tree canopy.

The interior is intended to create a forum for events and the promise of open discussion.
A ramp rises gently creating a promenade up through the pavilion for the visitor.

world. Affect becomes active rather than passive in the midst of encounters between all kinds of bodies: architectural bodies, natural bodies, bodies of water and air, and human and animal bodies. The provocation to a positive activation of affect is managed by Eliasson through quite simple means: the calculated distribution of light that is captured, projected and reflected; the management of water that is more or less fluid or viscous, even frozen. These means, as well as so many ephemera of duration, allow being to exfoliate as becoming so that fixed subjectivities can transform within a living world. We pass into the landscape as the landscape passes through us. Eliasson insists: 'I am not so interested in temporality, except as it relates to being part of the world.' The experiments he undertakes are not for the sake of mere art; they aspire to offer new kinds of engagement with a world fraught with social and environmental concerns. The question of individual and collective spatial experience in a world, and how this can be manifested through interior atmosphere, is fundamental to Eliasson's ongoing experimentation. ∆

Text © 2008 John Wiley & Sons Ltd. Images: pp 30-1 © Courtesy H&F Patronage, donated to Museum Boijmans van Beuningen, photo Jens Ziehe; p 32(t) © Ari Magg; p 32(b) © Courtesy Olafur Eliasson; Tanya Bonakdar, New York; neugerriemschneider, Berlin; p 33 © Courtesy BMW Group; p 34 © Courtesy Victor Pinchuk Foundation, photo Jens Ziehe; p 35(t) © Olafur Eliasson and Kjetil Thorsen, photo Luke Hayes; p 35(b) © Olafur Eliasson and Kjetil Thorsen, photo Luke Hayes

Affecting Data

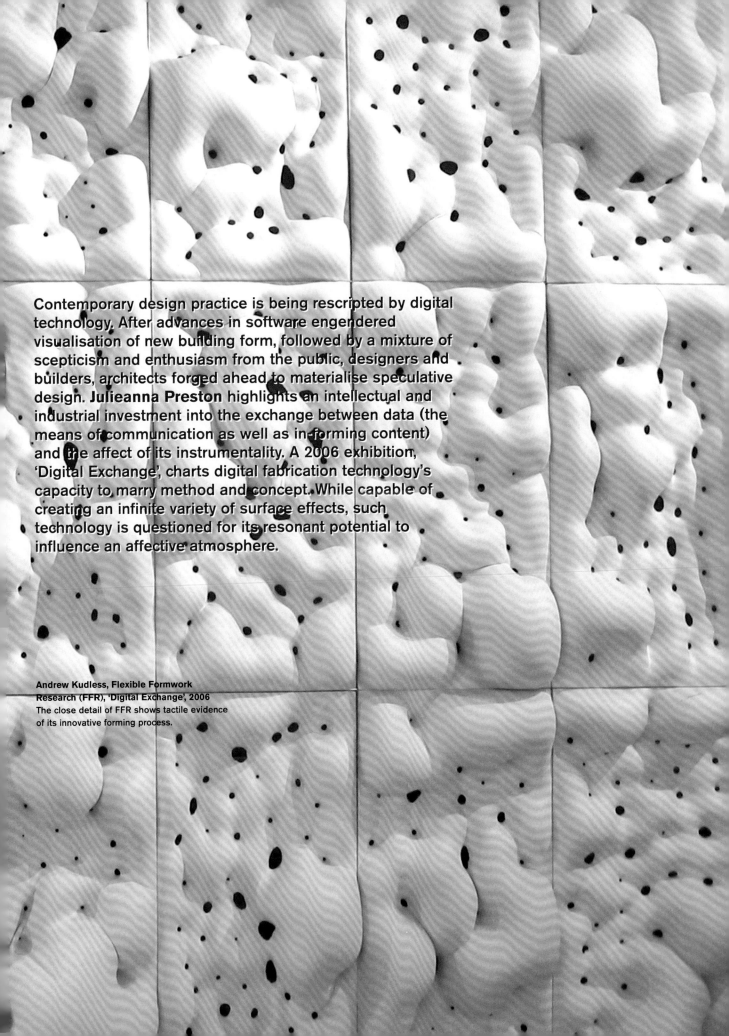

Contemporary design practice is being rescripted by digital technology. After advances in software engendered visualisation of new building form, followed by a mixture of scepticism and enthusiasm from the public, designers and builders, architects forged ahead to materialise speculative design. **Julieanna Preston** highlights an intellectual and industrial investment into the exchange between data (the means of communication as well as in-forming content) and the affect of its instrumentality. A 2006 exhibition, 'Digital Exchange', charts digital fabrication technology's capacity to marry method and concept. While capable of creating an infinite variety of surface effects, such technology is questioned for its resonant potential to influence an affective atmosphere.

Andrew Kudless, Flexible Formwork
Research (FFR), 'Digital Exchange', 2006
The close detail of FFR shows tactile evidence
of its innovative forming process.

If digitally fabricated architectural rescripts links between ideation and production, what is the impact of post-production? What is the performative affect of such technological effects?

In 1992, Peter Eisenman probed the impact of digital media on architectural design in an *AD* feature entitled 'The Affects of Singularity'. In his text, 'effect', the product of an agent or cause, is differentiated from 'affect', the 'sensate response to a physical environment'. Eisenman argues that several significant shifts towards the notion of reality challenge our ability to encounter affect or, better, atmosphere. As electronic mediated environments emerge from the vestiges of classicist organic, anthropomorphic and mechanical paradigms, architecture serves its utilitarian rather than its symbolic functions. 'The more the effective nature of the mechanism became the less the affective nature of both the medium and the message; the social and the political replaced the metaphorical or the affective type.' Accordingly, Eisenman credits singularity as distinctly different from individuality and particularity, with the potential to subvert the electronic paradigm. Singularity is the product of collective behaviour, an affinity for the subjective over formal and physical features.[1]

This plea for singularity over the standard repetitive norm the self-expressive individual and the technocratic mediated environment, serves as a means to measure contemporary digital fabrication design. More than a decade after Eisenman's text, numerous architects and designers have forged a dramatic shift from highly speculative designs shrouded in seductive glossy graphics of virtual and hypothetical space to highly specified architectural constructions invested with new systems and logics of shared communication, building processes and, of course, forms foreign to architecture's canonical vocabulary. Famous and familiar figures responsible for such advances include Greg Lynn,

Kevin Klinger and Gregory Luhan, 'Digital Exchange' exhibition, The Yard, Louisville, Kentucky, 2006
Each container was fitted with a flexible support system of CNC-milled plywood panels and lighting frames which enhanced the spatial effects of the display and illuminated the installation.

A reclaimed urban infill site is transformed by displays of digital fabrication housed in containers. The atmosphere of the opening night capitalises on the power of lighting, shadow and the heightened energy of the gathering crowd.

Frank Gehry and Mark Goulthorpe to name just a few. While the majority of this work primarily refigures the external envelope, designers such as Kol/Mac, SHoP and Asymptote have made significant contributions specific to interiors.[2] It appears from the mounting body of such work that digital technology and its associated fabrication is having an impact on how we imagine and build interiors, and their accompanying atmospheres. Understanding data as matter that oscillates within G-code and representational communication suggests that there is more to novel surfaces and forms than material manipulation: the work is capable of invoking spatial phenomena.

In October 2006 an international juried exhibition entitled 'Digital Exchange' opened as part of the ACADIA Synthetic Landscapes Conference at The Yard, a temporarily reclaimed urban infill site owned by the New Center for Contemporary Art in Louisville, Kentucky. The exhibition consisted of 30 design works installed within shipping containers. According to co-curators Kevin Klinger (director of the Institute for Digital Fabrication in the Center for Media Design and associate professor of architecture at Ball State University) and Gregory Luhan (associate dean for research at the University of Kentucky College of Design and a research fellow at the Center for Visualization and Virtual Environment): 'Digital technology facilitates navigation in and out of the boundaries of traditional architectural practice, and as such has rescripted our modes of production. As digital technology continues to form key linkages between the ideation process and the reality of production, alternate forms of practice in the design disciplines emerge ... transforming traditional modes of representing ideas into materials that further inform methods of making. As questions that relate to surface, interface and performance begin to emerge in relation to this digital exchange, it is undetermined which principles will

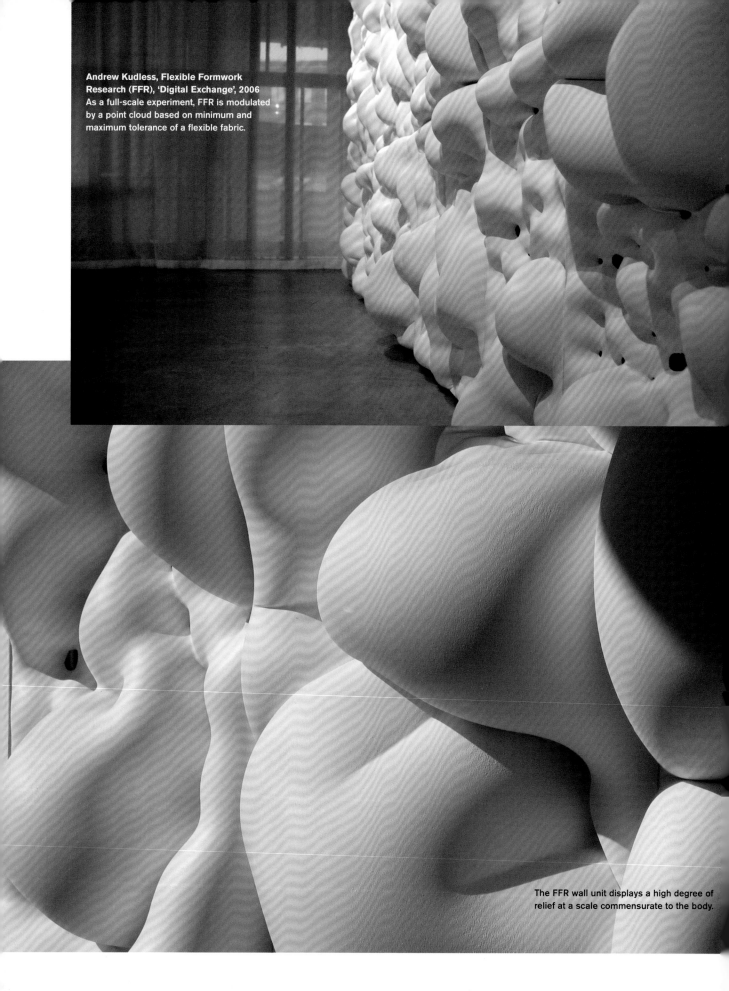

Andrew Kudless, Flexible Formwork Research (FFR), 'Digital Exchange', 2006
As a full-scale experiment, FFR is modulated by a point cloud based on minimum and maximum tolerance of a flexible fabric.

The FFR wall unit displays a high degree of relief at a scale commensurate to the body.

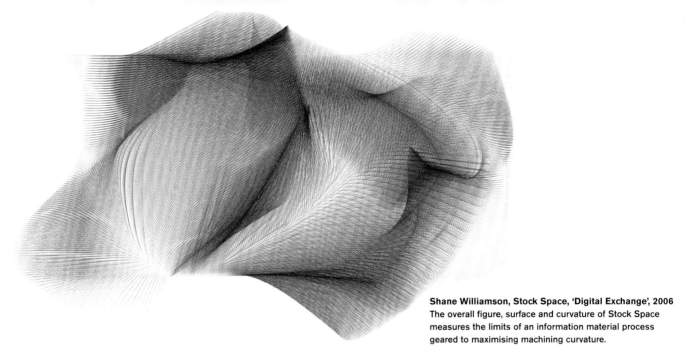

Shane Williamson, Stock Space, 'Digital Exchange', 2006
The overall figure, surface and curvature of Stock Space measures the limits of an information material process geared to maximising machining curvature.

The assemblage of stacked modules reveals traits of the isoparametric machining process.

The industrial size, economy and ease of modelling of rigid foam lend it to the work's greater tactile and acoustic properties.

exactly govern the development of the digital model, its resulting form, and spatial quality.' The review here considers the spatial impact of such informing practices.

Collectively, the works reiterate a rampant fascination in architectural design to embrace digital fabrication technology, much of which has resulted in a limitless number of gratuitous form-making projects. The 'Digital Exchange' exhibition probes deeper into architectural practice where all forms of information are as supple as the materials they manipulate. While still form-conscious, the designers respond to a full compendium of environmental and material factors, and as a result reflect a degree of complexity matched by a belief in data as a heterogeneously mediating medium. The age-old tiresome arguments between craft and industry are forsaken for a future where digital design development is privileged. Three of the exhibited works are especially pertinent to our discussion on atmosphere.

Flexible Formwork Research (FFR) by Andrew Kudless builds on the work of Spanish architect Miguel Fisac to investigate 'the self-organisation of plaster and elastic fabric to produce evocative visual and acoustic effects'. The project resonates with the body and our natural attraction and repulsion for certain forms: 'It unintentionally reminds us of our own flesh as it sags, expands, and wrinkles in relationship with gravity, structure, and time.'

Meanwhile, Shane Williamson's design, Stock Space, investigates the economy of engineering multiple modular units of high-density EPS foam 'capable of recording the vestigial marks of fabrication as well as providing adequate dampening and insulation'. Originally installed in a large convention centre, 'Stock Space was small, vertical, warm, and quiet, in contrast to the immense horizontality of the mechanically cooled trade floor of nearly 40,000 exhibitors and attendees'. This highly differentiated soft form challenges any sense of machine aesthetics.

Finally, Kevin Klinger outlines a collaborative project carried out with industry partners and architecture students enrolled at the Virginia B Ball Center for Creative Inquiry: 'The

Kevin Klinger, Calibration Channel, 'Digital Exchange', 2006
The Calibration Channel interior is constructed from a series of hybridised timber frames lined with red oak and ash planks.

Sited among a stand of deciduous trees, the Calibration Channel serves as an acoustic instrument to the river beyond.

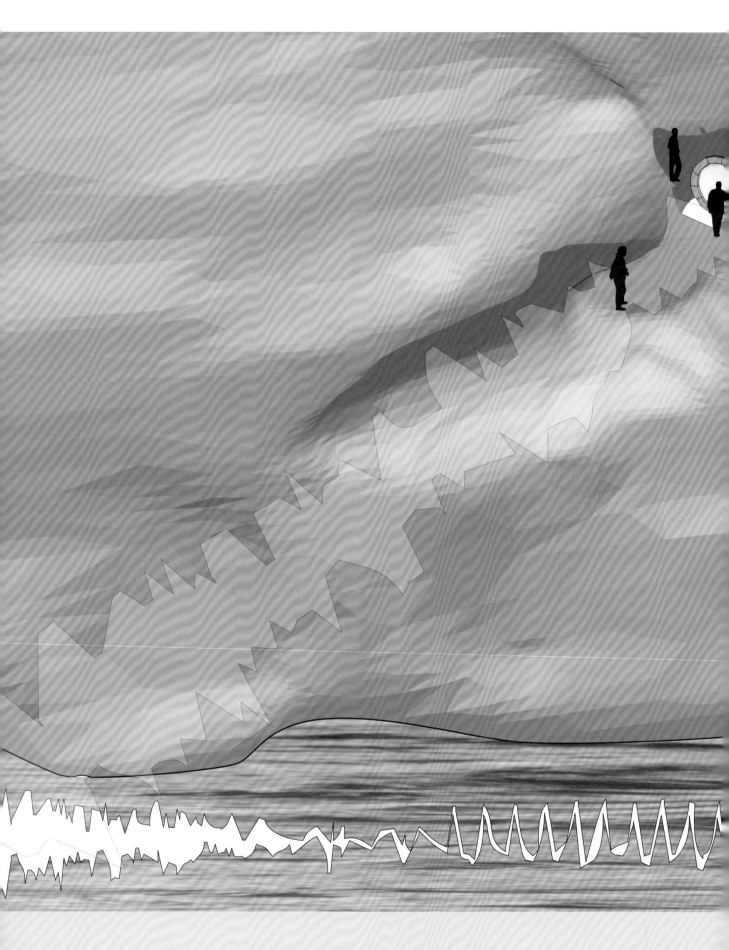

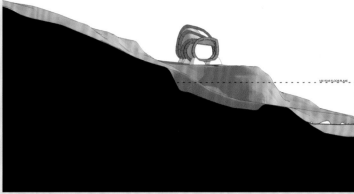

Perched on a terrace beyond the reach of a river's flood,
it is also a threshold in the landscape.

Calibration Channel provides a seating platform that channels
the river sounds in a manner that enables small groups and
individuals to undergo sensory calibration. Primary ribs,
digitally defined from the simulation models, contour an
interior skin, which acts as a secondary structural element.
This allowed for a smoother surface that would better
accommodate acoustics. The drawings and full-scale
construction reveal an intense planning process that sought
to maximise use of precious materials and enhance detail
resolution only made possible by data management. As an
instrument, the Calibration Channel acoustically tuned one's
body to the river beyond the visual.[3]

The 'Digital Exchange' curators defend the experimental
nature of the works in this exhibition as levers towards
expanding architectural practice. That they find digital media
and collaborative processes as critical agents to overturn long-
established practices that privilege authenticity, mastery and
formal expression is evidence that data could shed
atmospheric light, literally and singularly.[4] △

Kevin Klinger, *Calibration Channel*, 'Digital Exchange', 2006
As an installation specific to site and occupation, the Calibration Channel is
geared towards aligning one's sensory energy – an acoustic experience.

Notes
1. Peter Eisenman, 'The Affects of Singularity', *AD Theory & Experimentation:
Architectural Ideas for Today and Tomorrow*, Vol 62, No 11/12, Nov/Dec 1992,
pp 43–5.
2. In addition, while not specific to digital fabrication technology indebted to
CNC or rapid prototype equipment, a host of new designers, such as Sheila
Kennedy and J Franco Voilich (KVA) and KieranTimberlake, have recently
explored the interface between architecture and electricity. See, for example,
PRAXIS, Journal of Writing and Building: New Technologies/New Architectures,
Issue 6, 2004.
3. Calibration Channel project team: Kevin Klinger (associate professor),
Robert Horner (project leader), Robert Beach, Austin Durbin, Melissa Funkey,
Jorie Garcia, Anne Jeffs, Katie Marinaro, Christopher Peli, Josh Reitz, Jeremy
Richmond and Chelsea Wait. Industry partners: Indiana Limestone Fabricators,
Frank Miller Lumber Co.
4. This text originated from several conversations with the curators and
authors of the work and from the exhibition catalogue: Gregory A Luhan (ed),
The Digital Exchange: An Exhibition of Digital Manufacture and Visualization,
ACADIA Publications (Mansfield, OH), 2006.

Multivalent Performance in the Work of Lewis.Tsurumaki.Lewis

Four recent built works by **Paul Lewis**, **Marc Tsurumaki** and **David J Lewis** of Lewis.Tsurumaki.Lewis (LTL Architects) document a practice of reconceptualising interior space as a site of innovative material surfaces assembled from the repetition of readily available elements. The goal in this work is to intensify and expand the impact of a reduced set of operations, asking less to be more, through the interweaving of functional engagements and material conditions.

LTL Architects, Xing Restaurant, New York, 2005
The restaurant uses two linear miles of laminated acrylic strips to make a single element that unifies the diverse areas of the space through a single recognisable figure. The acrylic wrapper forms the bar top in the front of the space, illuminates the main dining area as a ceiling chandelier, and becomes the walls and doors for the bathrooms beyond.

LTL Architects approaches the transformation of interior spaces by designing projects that demonstrate what the practice calls 'multivalent performance'. In short, multivalent performance refers to the objective of producing work that navigates the divergent and often contradictory obligations of each project, a methodology that requires that the final design negotiate between the overlapping agendas of programme, spatial form and inhabitation while creating a sensory environment that engages the user at diverse levels.

Such architecture operates simultaneously at a rich haptic and optical level while sponsoring a dense range of uses, environmental functions and social conditions, often with a single space, form or surface.

Such architecture operates simultaneously at a rich haptic and optical level while sponsoring a dense range of uses, environmental functions and social conditions, often with a single space, form or surface. To create such work requires an aggressive reconceptualisation of interior space that moves quickly beyond the traditional categories and conventional understanding that are typically limited to floor-wall-ceiling nomenclatures. These categories of thought dominate and orchestrate most commercial approaches to the interior, demarcated and classified through the drawing conventions of plan, elevation and reflected ceiling plan. The work of LTL seeks to confound spatial expectations through a playful engagement of conventions, one that foregrounds volumetric definitions and encourages oscillations between surface delineation, material construction and use.

As an architecture firm committed to the vitality of the city through the reoccupation and reuse of existing buildings, LTL has developed a proactive methodology towards architectural practice within the interior environment, one demonstrated and tested through a series of recent projects. Many of these are located within existing interior volumes in New York City, mostly accessible at street level as former shop fronts, where the basic framework and boundaries for work are the legacy of past occupation and construction. The question posed by these conditions is how to use the limitations and constraints of the given spaces as a catalyst for design.

While in many cases the final interior design, driven by an insistence on multivalent performance, may result in a space that is perceived by the user to demonstrate atmosphere, it is not the primary goal of LTL's design process. Atmosphere is a quality of space residing in the observer, and is not intrinsic to the space itself. One attributes the description 'atmosphere' to spaces and events if they are perceived to be deviations from the normal or everyday – a foggy day, for instance – creating conditions in which the viewer becomes

LTL Architects, Ini Ani Coffee Shop, New York, 2004
Ini Ani Coffee Shop defines a volume within a volume through the stacking of 5-centimetre (2-inch) thick cut cardboard framed within cold-rolled steel to create an acoustically appropriate and inviting room for daily patrons to linger. Cast plaster coffee-cup lids mark the entry space, turning the prosaic into a display event.

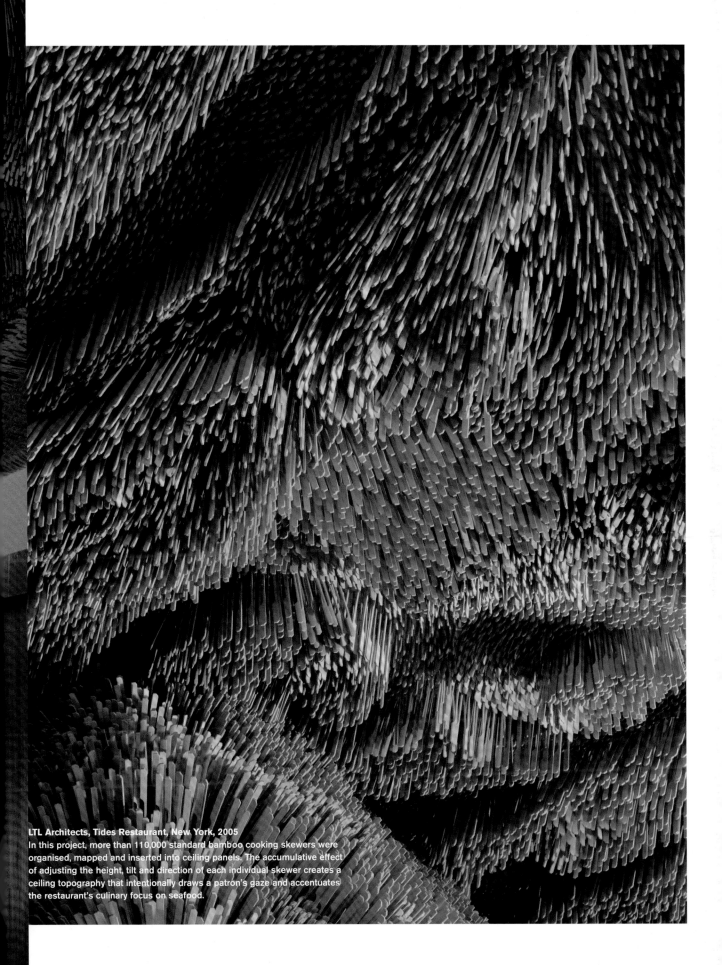

LTL Architects, Tides Restaurant, New York, 2005
In this project, more than 110,000 standard bamboo cooking skewers were organised, mapped and inserted into ceiling panels. The accumulative effect of adjusting the height, tilt and direction of each individual skewer creates a ceiling topography that intentionally draws a patron's gaze and accentuates the restaurant's culinary focus on seafood.

LTL Architects, New York University Office of Strategic Assessment, Planning and Design, New York, 2007
A single inserted element extending the length of the space meets the primary architectural obligations of the Office of Strategic Assessment, Planning and Design. This hybrid wall + ceiling component provides privacy for the offices and creates a clear circulation zone granting divergent display needs at each end.

The industrial felt absorbs sound and draws an occupant's view through the length of the space, providing a self-healing material for temporary installations and exhibitions.

self-conscious about his or her surroundings. While LTL's work may illicit such responses, this is the result of a more thorough and tactical approach to the specific performative requirements of the project. Yet, if the sense of atmosphere is perceived in the work or space, it is likely to be produced in the play between the familiar and the uncanny through the tactic of constructing surfaces and interior environments through the repetition of ordinary elements. In the case of material repetition, inexpensive and readily available materials are combined to produce complex composite surfaces. The rich spatial and visual qualities of these assemblies belie their prosaic origin, creating optical patterns and tactile qualities that induce perceptual oscillation between the individual component and the overall field. Up close, the individual component is recognisable while the overall surface is unintelligible, but from a distance new patterns and effects exceed the legibility of the single piece.

This use of repetition is at play in a series of the practice's recent interior projects, from office spaces to a series of restaurants, including New York University's Office of Strategic Assessment, Planning and Design, Xing Restaurant, Tides Restaurant and the Ini Ani Coffee Shop. In each, the design of the plans and overall organisation of the projects were set by the programme in order to maximise seating while ensuring an efficiency of circulation. The challenge in each of these projects was how to maximise the impact and engagement of the surfaces that remain. Here, LTL approached these surfaces as opportunities for material construction, and not simply sites for product specification, thus defining the spaces through an aggregation of industrial felt, painted plywood slats, cut cardboard, cast plaster, acrylic strips and bamboo skewers. The goal was to intensify and expand the impact of a reduced set of operations, asking less to be more, through the interweaving of functional engagements and material conditions. ∆

Condensation

Regionalism and the Room in John Yeon's Watzek House

Mary Anne Beecher's discussion of Aubrey Watzek's house extends traditional notions of regionalism to the domain of the interior. She outlines numerous ways that the local landscape and history figure as condensed renditions within rooms, surfaces and details. It is here that we find evidence of interior atmosphere developed as identity within a specific cultural and geographical context.

Interior spaces said to have atmosphere may seem rare today perhaps because most people seldom have an opportunity to escape the generic world. In fact, much of today's interior architecture has little notoriety due to the rising tide of homogeneity that has flooded most contemporary building practices. However, by expressing the properties of particular surroundings or environments, interior rooms may distinguish themselves from those that form the backdrop for everyday experiences. In this way, atmosphere may be created.

If atmosphere is, at least in part, the expression of locality, then determining whether or not a room seems to belong where it is situated is one way to identify its presence. Such a space expresses a connection to its larger setting. In this way atmosphere is cultivated by the use of particular spatial qualities, constructed views, and a definable palette of materials drawn from a particular locale. Interiors that capture these qualities may be perceived as condensed renditions of landscape that reinforce the association of a room to its surroundings – its building, site, and perhaps even its region. Such spaces heighten the experience of a more broadly known place by concentrating an array of its essential elements into a single room or series of rooms.

Regionalism is a framework that is often used to distinguish the traits of designs that are particular to their location. Regionalist expressions of architectural design capitalise on relationships established by a place with its climate, resident cultural practices and the materials at hand in patterns that are both predictable and fluid over time. The patterns used to define a region's architectural vocabulary, however, are more commonly based on exterior characteristics such as form and cladding, or on organisational principles

John Yeon, Watzek House, Portland, Oregon, 1937
The roof forms and narrow columns of Yeon's design for the Watzek House exterior establish an expression of locality by mirroring the distant mountain peaks and the tall Douglas firs on the site.

By incorporating irregular plantings and water into the geometry of the courtyard, Yeon encouraged visitors to establish connections between the natural elements of the site and the internal constructed spaces of the house.

such as plan type. For instance, in the Pacific Northwest region of the US, the climate (moderate and rainy) and the landscape (open valleys and conifer-covered volcanic mountains) together contribute to the creation of a distinctive image of regional architecture made up of heavy timber buildings with rough-textured surfaces and deep overhangs.

Thematic 'Northwest' rooms are often punctuated by the presence of heavy timber columns, log-lined walls and Native American blankets and pottery. Their colour schemes reflect nature's palette of mossy green and rusty cedar.

Because interiors have come to be perceived as independent and temporary entities within buildings, the extent to which they reflect their locale is a rare lens through which to examine them. Instead, rooms are often defined by aesthetic effects created by surface treatments that are usually understood as transient. The analysis of such characteristics has historically yielded identification with a recognised yet independent system of decorative styles. For instance, when the heaviness and textures of the Pacific Northwest design vocabulary are applied to interiors, these rugged qualities are more likely to be interpreted as clichéd themes that conjure images of logging camps or fishing

cabins. Thematic 'Northwest' rooms are often punctuated by the presence of heavy timber columns, log-lined walls and Native American blankets and pottery. Their colour schemes reflect nature's palette of mossy green and rusty cedar. But perhaps because we have come to anticipate the thematic room in isolation from its literal surroundings, such spaces often fail to resonate as authentic or meaningful, and thus may be said to lack 'atmosphere' – at least as it is reflected in the work of John Yeon.

The interiors of Yeon's 1937 house for Oregon lumberman Aubrey Watzek exemplify the expression of atmosphere in part due to their ability to transcend the clichés of Pacific Northwest design. When the curators at New York's Museum of Modern Art (MoMA) included the Watzek House in the exhibition 'Built in the USA: 1932–1944' and its accompanying publication, they placed it in the company of the nation's most significant works of Modern architecture. Elizabeth Mock, Alfred Farr and Philip L Goodwin selected the house for this exhibition because of Yeon's skilful execution of modern design principles, such as his careful siting of the building and his use of geometric forms. By highlighting these design features, they reinforced its similarity to classic designs by the better-known European Modernists Walter Gropius and Mies van der Rohe, while disregarding the significance of its interior spaces.

The exterior of the Watzek House reflects a combination of abstract Modernism and vernacular regionalism. The roofline of the house, located in Portland, echoes the snow-capped peak of Mount Hood seen in the distance, and the narrow columns outside the living room's terrace overhang reflect the verticality of the site's numerous surrounding fir trees. Still, Yeon's use of modern details like flush horizontal fir siding,

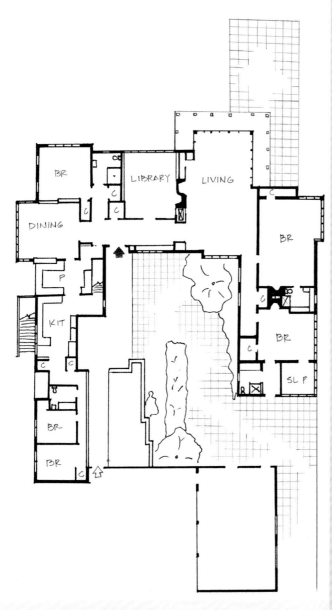

Yeon's use of the entrance hall allows the experience of distant views of the primary spaces that hint at, but do not fully disclose, each room's character and detail.

the expansive use of glass on the elevation oriented towards the view, and the rigid application of a grid to organise the landscape and the placement of the house within it, avoid connections to the more 'unrefined' traits of stereotypical Northwestern design.

Despite the dismissal of the relevance of interiors of the Watzek House by the exhibition's curators, it is Yeon's orchestration of volumes that more deeply reflects the house' regionalism and expresses the essence of condensation. The floor plan reveals that its interior spaces are oriented around a circulation spine that choreographs what Yeon himself described as 'a sequence of revelations'[1] that is not unlike a walk through an Oregon forest. When Watzek had his house built in this area of west Portland, there were few surrounding structures in a relatively dense landscape. Over the years, encroaching houses and increasingly mature plantings have reshaped the character of the neighbourhood.

Although the most important attributes of the relationship between the house, its rooms and the building's site have survived this transition, photographs taken at the time of the building's completion capture the fullest extent of Yeon's intent.

Although the most important attributes of the relationship between the house, its rooms and its site have survived this transition, photographs taken at the time of the building's completion capture the fullest extent of Yeon's intent. Then and now, the interiors benefit from vistas that shift from the dining room's intimate views of a native shade garden to the living room's sweeping floor-to-ceiling framed view of Mount Hood, offering stimulating variation and a comforting reassurance of the fitness of these spaces to the land that lies beyond them.

One enters the Watzek House by first passing through a courtyard that operates very much like an outdoor room. Here, the primacy of the landscape is introduced and the geometry of the spatial layout established. A large reflecting pool mirrors the colours and movements of the courtyard's plantings while the flagstones on its floor establish a gridded plane that extends (by implication) through the house to the living room terrace on its opposite side.

To reach the public rooms, one must pass through the entry hall. Yeon's design for the entrance is a compressed corridor that connects the major public spaces of the house. Metaphorically, the spatial compression of the entry hall reflects the contrast between the density of the forest's edge and the openness of western Oregon's field-filled valley with its numerous rivers and lakes. It enhances the sense of exposure created by the Watzek House courtyard and its primary public spaces: the dining room and the living room. By leading occupants through a darker, more enclosing space first, Yeon successfully exaggerates the volume of the moderately scaled rooms intended to form backdrops for social gatherings.

One end of the entrance corridor terminates in the dining room. Here, the relatively small room visually expands by reaching out into the landscape through an expansive floor-to-ceiling bay window. The atmosphere of the room is established by this tenuous edge and playful light that trickles in through the tree branches. Yeon also includes custom-designed elements such as a sculptural central chandelier and a built-in buffet that, as three suspended boxes, references the repetitive square motif found in spaces throughout the house. The round, dish forms of the chandelier and the recessed semicircular handles for each section of the cabinet soften the room's rigidity without lessening its geometry.

The other end of the entrance corridor leads to the living room that Wallace Kay Huntington memorably described as 'the room that belongs to the mountain'.[2] This room, with its 4.3-metre (14-foot) high coffered ceiling and panelled walls, condenses the region's spatial extremes into a single area. Wax-rubbed vertical-grained noble fir panelling wraps the

Just off the entrance hall, the rhythmic design of the library roots the house in its location by expressing integration with the inclusion of custom cabinet pulls and built-in furniture.

The darkened spaces under the canopy of extending branches beyond the dining room are echoed in the recesses and projections seen in Yeon's custom cabinetry designs.

The living room balances the luminous quality of the glass face as it turns towards Mount Hood with the reflective radiance of its wax-rubbed fir surfaces.

The living room captures the landscape's extremes by mediating between the controlle courtyard vegetation, seen through a framed and the wide-open views of the mountain rar to the east on the opposite side of the room.

The living room ceiling wraps its inhabitants in warmth and expresses the subtle texture and colour variations that encapsulate the Oregon landscape.

room in the warm colours and varied textures of Oregon's landscape. The darker, more internal side of the space echoes the enclosure of a forest's vegetation by incorporating a small seating area within the room's implied circulation space. Here, from a chair turned inwards, Aubrey Watzek could enjoy a view of the more intimately scaled courtyard.

The bright open end of the room is more like the valley floor, lined with warm honey-coloured panels and flooded with light. The grid of the wall and ceiling panels extends the rhythm of the thin window mullions and the slender columns beyond them throughout the room. A smooth marble mantel in the sidewall repeats the module while introducing a softening curve to the otherwise rigid plane.

While the varied volumes and beautiful materials of the Watzek House interiors reflect characteristic qualities of the Pacific Northwest landscape, Yeon, a lifelong student of Oregon's landscape, recognised that the distinction of a place resides in its details. It is, therefore, in the detailing of the rooms that the subtleties of the landscape are captured and expressed in a manner that results in the creation of atmosphere. For instance, as the rectangular wall panels accentuate the room's verticality, the square ceiling panels alternate in their grain direction. Divided by a series of feather-thin beams, these ceiling panels form a light and rhythmic horizontal counterbalance to the walls.

The integration of built-in features in nearly every room also elevates the role of the detail in the expression of a condensed landscape here. In addition to a pair of hidden storage closets in the living room wall, on either side of the fireplace and the dining room buffet Yeon included built-in cabinetry that expresses the geological characteristics of the Northwest region's landscape, where the earth's shifting plates frequently interrupt rivers and streams to create cascading waterfalls, and rocky outgrowths of lava ring the shores of mountain lakes. His built-ins provide the sense that the interior elements of the house are integrated with its structure as a reminder that despite the regional landscape's propensity for movement via its various forms of water, there is still, at the base of it all, an overt terra firma.

It may be argued that industrialisation and globalisation have greatly diminished the ability of today's designers to generate an authentic regionalism. Yet after 70 years the integration of naturally finished local materials with custom architectural elements that preserves and enhances views of nature in Yeon's Watzek House still evokes the Oregon landscape with a timeless series of rooms that seem to belong where they are. As a model for how atmosphere might be created in contemporary interiors, Yeon's subtle use of materials and the manipulation of scale offer a strong argument for the value of constructing abstracted regionalist designs that do not rely on the literal to evoke a sense of the extraordinary. ⌂

Notes
1. Dan Hortsch, 'Nationally-known architectural designer dies', *The Oregonian*, 15 March 1996, p L4.
2. Wallace Kay Huntington, 'Parks and gardens of Western Oregon', in Thomas Vaughn (ed), *Space, Style and Structure, Buildings in Northwest America*, Oregon Historical Society, 1974, p 570.

Walter Pichler's House Next to the Smithy

Atmosphere and Ground

Approaching atmosphere from a cultural perspective, **Paul James** explores conceptions of ground in a work by the Austrian architect, sculptor and draughtsman Walter Pichler. Where atmosphere relates to the critical strategy of clouding, to render obscure, to resist rhetorical clarity, Pichler's House Next to the Smithy, documented in drawings and photographs, highlights a link between weather and atmosphere, and darkness and interiority.

Walter Pichler, *Träumer (Dreamer)*, painting, 2002
The person sleeping recalls the skeletal figure in Félicien Rops' frontispiece for Baudelaire's *Epaves* of 1866.

Atmosphere relates to the critical strategy of clouding, to render obscure, to resist rhetorical clarity.

Walter Pichler, House Next to the Smithy, South Tyrol, Italy, 1995–2002
Access to the cellar is through a trap door located in front of the entrance to the living quarters.

The word 'atmosphere' can denote the prevailing psychological climate. There is a connection between atmosphere, as an image of the density of embodied spatial experience, and the notion of a worldview or horizon. Martin Heidegger argued that we perceive the world through various horizons, which can be religious, moral, ideological, aesthetic and psychological. It is through these categories, he argued, that we interpret the sense and purpose of existence and history. Atmosphere is the spatial field through which we encounter and subsequently represent the world. This contribution explores the connection between atmosphere as a form of horizon and atmosphere as a physical phenomenon, and argues that architecture can provide a representation of the latent cultural content of a site, which can be read through the prereflective experience of interior atmosphere.

In 1994, Pichler's cousin (also called Walter Pichler) commissioned the house next to the workshop of their grandfather, a blacksmith, when the smithy was being restored and was under a recent conservation order. The client's father, Pichler's uncle, Eugen, was the last blacksmith to have worked there. The smithy is no longer used and now functions as a historic record of the family's presence on the site, rather than as a utilitarian structure. The house was designed for short-term accommodation for Pichler's friends and family.

In 2003, Pichler wrote an account of his relationship to the site of the building, which is located within the Eggental Valley in South Tyrol, Italy.[1] His family left the valley in 1941, prompted by the Hitler–Mussolini accord, and emigrated to North Tyrol. Pichler was then five years old and later recalled both his and his mother's distress as they were forced to leave the valley. He returned to the valley on various occasions as a child and remembers the old smithy affectionately. His stated aim for the project was to place memory on an equal footing with solid material. Memory is intended to transform the past rather than to simply recall it. The building represents Pichler's relationship to the site, setting up a dialogue with both the original memory and the smithy itself.

The central importance of memory within this project connects to his broader practice as a sculptor and architect. Since the 1970s Pichler has created site-specific sculptures, and buildings to house them within his farm in St Martin in Burgenland, Austria. He consistently attempts to create an intimate dialogue between his sculptures and the site within which they are located. The formal language of his architecture is dominated by moments of either resisting or merging with the ground.

The Binary of the Interior

Atmosphere relates to the critical strategy of clouding, to render obscure, to resist rhetorical clarity. The House Next to the Smithy contains two floors: one above ground containing living quarters, and one below ground containing a wine cellar. These are linked by a semisubmerged corridor, which is capped significantly by foundation stones. The design has a diagrammatic clarity that is complicated by Pichler's emphasis on cycles and flows between states.

There are no penetrations in the walls of the house. The building is double-skinned with a row of unmortared coping stones placed over the gap between these layers. In order to reach the cellar one must progress through a trap door, and then navigate a narrow corridor surmounted by monumental boulders sourced from the nearby river. This heightens awareness of the progression into subterranean space. The foundation rocks give hierarchical importance to this space. The corridor is a space of movement between thresholds. The space speaks of transition in multiple terms, most obviously from terrain to subterranean space and light to dark. But this space also resounds existentially as a rehearsal of the subject's eventual mergence with primordial ground.

The foundation rocks spanning the subterranean corridor signal the importance of the liminal within Pichler's poetics.

View of the corridor space leading to the cellar.

Conflicting signs dominate Pichler's poetics. The negative cultural projections upon dark space are alluded to alongside imagery that refers to the privileged insight of the melancholic. The outer walls of the corridor envelop the cellar, which lies completely beneath the ground, totally submerged. Its spatial qualities are highly evocative of the anxiety that Anthony Vidler identifies with 'Dark Space'. In his eponymous essay,[2] Vidler summarised the associations with light and dark in the context of the Enlightenment. During the Enlightenment, the primary identification with light and dark spaces was moral. Light spaces were aligned with the health of the individual and, by extension, the social body. Light released society from the dark forces of myth and folklore. Dark space, in contrast, was aligned with the pathological, the unseen and the diseased agent that will harm the social body.

Countering the Enlightenment connection between light and access to truth is the historic connection between melancholia and insight. Darkness structures the melancholic's encounter with the world through his or her sensitivity to the opacity of representation. In her essay on Pichler, Diane Lewis tied him to the tradition of darkness rather than light.[3] She suggested that the visible is an unreliable source of information and that there is a deeper structure that would be more accessible with either the removal or the repression of the visible. The melancholic is conscious of the impossibility of objective knowledge of the appearance of the world. In response to the resulting descent into the abyss of subjectivism and relativism, the melancholic reconceptualises the material world as a mask.

Pichler has constructed a space for perception through a repression of the visible. His denial of views of the landscape and the extensive use of dark space is significant in this context as he attempts to transcend an ocular-centric experience of landscape. This highly internalised spatial condition is one of the strategies he uses to rearticulate site and ground. The specific qualities of site are exchanged for the abstract experience of time and duration, provided by various cycles including the cycle from light to darkness, of the seasons, and the longer life cycle evident in the physical breakdown and decay of our bodies as we age.

We experience history through atmosphere. The exaggeration of weather in Pichler's building foregrounds the experience of time within the interior. Weather is received rather than resisted by the building. Rain falls between the coping stones into the corridor before seeping back to the river. The gently sloping roof collects snow that is melted by the heat of the chimney breast. Precipitation collects in a drainage basin at the foot of the chimney before being discharged, like the rain, into the river. In part, the abstract experience of site is provided by the shifting shadow patterns formed by the roof's structure. Throws of light enter the space. Complex patterns are created by different densities of snow and rain that are registered within the interior by flickering shadows.

Fallen Nature

In architects' drawings, the ground plane is often represented as a thin line with blank space beneath it. Pichler represents the ground as a dense emotively loaded substance in tension with architecture through building design and drawing. He alludes to traditions that attribute authenticity to the ground, both Christian and pagan, and to the imagery of the Symbolist poets who viewed nature as an empty husk. His drawings activate a specific cultural understanding of landscape that is tied to the concept of ground as origin.

Stone is an emblem of permanence. Pichler counters this association by representing his building with a skeletal figure within the landscape, in order to allude to the emblematic role of his buildings as a sign of the human subject's inevitable submission to natural history. The figure in the foreground has a marked similarity to images of nature as having 'fallen', produced during the late 19th century. During this period there was a large increase in atheism in the West, particularly among the intellectual classes. In the Christian theory of nature, God was viewed as the Creator of the natural world. The splendour of the natural world was seen as evidence of God's existence. Nature was therefore viewed as meaningful due to its connection to the Creator. With the rise of atheism, artists began to represent nature as a ruin – as an entity that was absent of meaning. Withered landscapes mirrored the new understanding of death as final, rather than as a moment of transition to a heavenly realm.

The house is designed to rehearse the process of its eventual dissipation; it provides a representation of a post-mythic concept of death that disputes the possibility of transcendence. Lying semisubmerged in the ground, there is the obvious implication that the smithy is sinking. The walls extend out beyond the low-pitched roof structure establishing a hierarchical relationship between these elements. The roof is placed upon the walls, appearing to rest there as a temporary protective element. The expressed gap between them suggests a moment of transition prior to roof failure when the wall, as ruin, remains.

The oblique elevation of the house and smithy expresses the significance of the building entrance. The entrance walls form a semicircle that delineates the space in front of the building, while low-lying sinking walls suggest an archaeological remnant. These entrance walls are rendered with the same fragility as the smithy they reach towards. In contrast to the more clearly rendered house, the faintly drawn smithy suggests a process of erasure within which the historic smithy is in a more advanced stage. Paper absorbs the pigment, echoing the ground's absorption of the building.

Pichler rearticulates site as ground by activating the latent cultural associations of the site. Atmosphere is the agent of change and the horizon through which conscious reflection upon experience is enacted. Weather, light and soil are reconfigured through his architecture into emblems of transformation that tie the body to primordial ground. This knowledge haunts and threatens the architectural structures that we erect to immortalise ourselves. Although Pichler attempts to inscribe his biography in the landscape, he is conscious of the futility of such an act. The non-negotiable fact that both our constructions and our selves will be erased is evident in his representations. ⊅

View of the living quarters. The connection between light and access to truth is complicated by the repression of views of the surrounding landscape.

The side elevation of the house represents both its proximity to the smithy within the site and their proximity within a temporal cycle.

Notes
1. Walter Pichler, 'Walter Pichler House Next to the Smithy', *A + U*, No 10 (397), 2003, p 8.
2. Anthony Vidler, 'Dark Space', *The Architectural Uncanny: Essays in the Modern Unhomely*, MIT (Cambridge, MA), 1992, pp 167–75.
3. Diane Lewis, *Walter Pichler: Drawings, Sculptures, Architecture*, Jung und Jung (Salzburg), 2001, p 7.

Bridging the Threshold of Interior and Landscape

An Interview with Petra Blaisse

In a design practice dedicated to fusing insides and outsides, Petra Blaisse converses with **Lois Weinthal** about the atmospheric calling of interior textiles. As curtains and floor coverings furnish programmatically organised interior environments, they reflect larger spatial and historic contexts to demonstrate a confluence of micro and macro scales.

Petra Blaisse/Inside Outside, Heemstra/Strik House, Amsterdam, The Netherlands, 2002
Pattern and colour are used here for the climate- and sound-regulating wall at the entry.

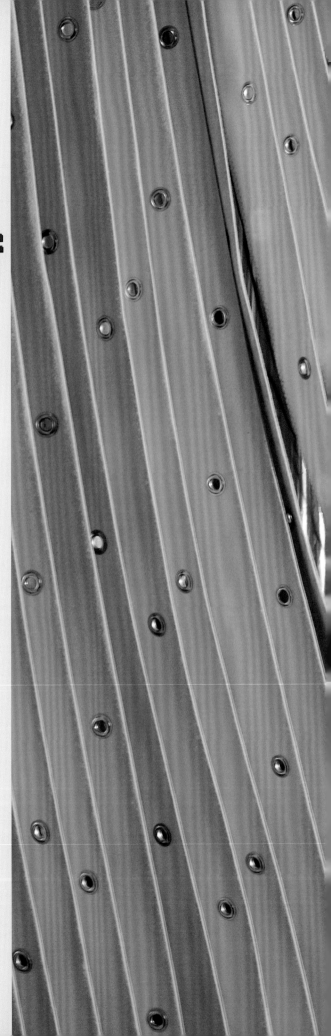

At the threshold of interior and exterior, Petra Blaisse bridges body, interior design, landscape design and architecture through textiles to create fluid atmospheres ranging from micro to macro scales. Projects by Blaisse and her office, Inside Outside located in Amsterdam, include large textiles inspired by clothing construction and iconography found in nature. Magnified to create oversized gardens within an interior, these designs are a reference to nature's orchestration of texture, colour and scent. Borrowing scales from inside and outside, Blaisse's atmospheres build upon the architectural structure, each reinterpreting the other. Inside Outside has undertaken a number of projects that include restorations such as the Hackney Empire theatre in London and collaboration with architectural offices including the Office for Metropolitan Architecture (OMA) on the Seattle Central Library, the Casa da Música in Portugal and The Netherlands Embassy in Berlin, and collaboration with graphic designer Bruce Mau.

The role of macro and micro is described by Blaisse as 'using both the language of the detail and the language of the whole, the entirety. All objects are made with the objective of taking both front and back sides as equally important; there is no hierarchy between near and far away. Each object or environment needs to catch the eye and trigger the senses from every perspective and position; screened or unscreened by glass facades or objects of some kind; preferably in every circumstance, time of day or night.'

Blaisse experiments with the potential of curtains, knowing the textile as a second skin to her own. As textiles are applied to both the body and architecture at different

Petra Blaisse/Inside Outside, Hackney Empire, London, 2005
Smocking detail inspired by clothing techniques alters the notion of the typical red theatre curtain.

The smocking detail applied to the theatre curtain at full scale.

scales, she notes a fluid connection between the two as 'cloth is soft and flexible and therefore it drapes itself around a person or object; or it falls down in swirls, folds or pleats, depending on the cloth's structure and weight. Fashion uses the properties of cloth and manipulates it to bring these properties to light, to achieve certain effects just as we do. I have always been interested in fashion as a form of architecture and art, as a way to create space or to envelop and take on a form. As in fashion, we consider both sides of a cloth equally important. But in our work, we do not drape the cloth around another shape: we let it hang down from a certain structure or form; it falls down, sways, moves sideways. Curtain and body touch each other only when the curtain is being pulled, pushed, lifted, moulded, rolled, stored, felt or stroked.' When placed in architecture, the curtain retains a sense of movement and challenges the static nature of architecture allowing the interior to reconfigure itself from permanent to dynamic.

For the renovation of the Hackney Empire in London, Blaisse refers to the smocking effect of clothing as a detail applied to the larger scale of a stage curtain. At the micro scale, a substructure gives pattern to the curtain, and when unfurled reveals a visual connection back to clothing. The idea of the curtain as clothing for architecture is further reinforced in the Casa da Música in Portugal. Layered curtains are placed at the perimeter of the concert hall taking on the effect of a veil to form a textural and visual relationship with the city, whether one is looking in or out. Because the curtains need to perform acoustically, they respond not only to the visual senses, but also to the audible. 'Textures often

Petra Blaisse/Inside Outside, Casa da Música, Porto, Portugal, 2005
The collaboration with OMA on this music hall project led to the installation of view filters – a series of layered screens on the interior facade allowing for light or dark when needed, responding to interior and exterior conditions.

have to do with programme: acoustic, light, view. But they are an aesthetic composition too. The scale of a texture is influenced by the context: the room, the environment, the technical programme for the space.'

At the Seattle Central Library, Blaisse captures the passage of time in the seasonal changes of gardens to construct a collection of visual and tactile experiences. As one traverses the spiral ramp, views open up to nature both inside and outside the library. The interior textiles reference the perimeter landscaping, where reading areas include floor textiles with oversized imagery taken from nature, reinforcing the dialogue between landscape and interior. Blaisse points out that 'micro and macro views are, of course, essential in Inside Outside's work: they illustrate – or point out – the scale and variety of the space the objects are part of, and also make the viewer aware of the different quality of the one close up and the other from a distance, not limiting anyone to one directed experience but introducing the entire gamut of possible experiences through one and the same thing.'

From the library's balcony levels, a view to the ground level affords a seamless connection between an exterior garden on one side and the digital representation of the garden woven into a carpet on the other, revealing a mirror image of one another. The glass wall, the architecture, divides nature and artifice to both dissolve their mutual boundaries and reinforce the visual fluidity between interior and exterior. Blaisse refers to the cyclic garden 'in the sense that there is an awareness of

change, climate and the influence of time, light, sound, temperature, moisture, draught, movement and decay'. Gardens reinforce the ability 'to follow the flow of things without interrupting and with acceptance of what comes', not dissimilar from the world of narratives in libraries that transport the reader to another geography.

Blaisse develops an identity for The Netherlands Embassy in Berlin by merging Dutch landscape iconography and traditions in textiles and weaving. The result is a variety of curtains responding to conditions as seen on both the inside and outside of the embassy. When asked about the connection between function and atmosphere, Blaisse says: 'Atmosphere in the literal sense is one of the functions that one requires from our objects or environments: acoustic, climatic, visual, light. Textures and patterns are also chosen for aesthetic reasons, although textures are more often programmed to catch light and sound waves, to allow them through or to absorb or scatter them. Patterns can do the same, as in direction and distance of yarn or the effect of 3-D forms and openings, but they – together with colour – are more often chosen to influence the experience of a place (its function, its scale) or to tell something about a place or about its direct environment: history, intention, cultural meaning or function of a building, fashion and moment in time.'

The types of processes and technologies Blaisse explores for the design and fabrication of textiles requires 'research into "new" techniques and materials, often to discover that these

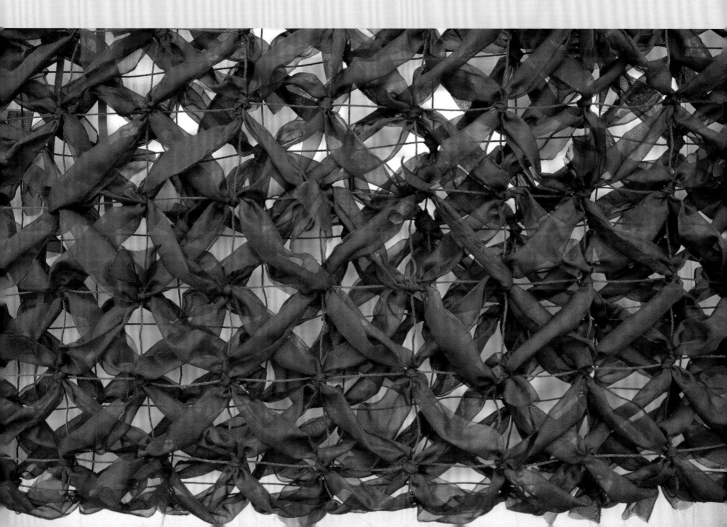

Petra Blaisse/Inside Outside, Seattle Central Library, Washington, US, 2004
Oversized garden imagery becomes the pattern for textile design in this building by OMA. The juxtaposition
of people and imagery further highlights the role of textiles at macro/micro scales.

The textile garden imagery on the interior meets garden on the exterior at the threshold of glass.

Petra Blaisse/Inside Outside, The Netherlands Embassy, Berlin, Germany, 2004
Blaisse collaborated with the Textile Museum in Tilburg to produce a classic jacquard technique, creating a double-sided damask linen. The pattern incorporates imagery from the Dutch landscape resulting in the overall design of a curtain that regulates light and sound in the interior.

are not (yet) applicable to our public building projects because of time, safety, wear, maintenance or budget reasons. We often start work along the lines of our instincts and experience that point us into certain directions for each situation and with each specific material. For complex issues such as precise acoustic, light, airflow or climatic measurements we invite specialists in the field to do the necessary analysis. As far as the designing of the cloth is concerned, we do a lot of classic things like weaving, knotting, knitting, tearing, cutting, melting, burning, shrinking, sewing, laser-cutting, lining, pleating, folding, adjusting, layering, quilting, stitching, gluing, ironing and starching.'

Blaisse synthesises micro and macro scales, forming complementary relationships that reveal that 'there are no inside outside spaces, there is only the illusion of inside outside spaces. To achieve this, our work must consist of at least two disciplines, both manifested inside and outside; intertwined, side by side, in the produced part of each other or taking each other's place.' ⚮

Off the Peg

The Bespoke Interiors of Ben Kelly

Ben Kelly Design, The Haçienda, Manchester, 1982
Once inside, the clubber emerged from the dark constrained entrance into the massive warehouse-type space. It was only at this point that the noise, sweat and frenetic energy became apparent.

Known for his unique ability to assemble disparate materials, colours and textures, interior designer Ben Kelly speaks with Graeme Brooker and Sally Stone about the ideas and intentions behind his work. His thoughts and works indicate a respect for revealing the underlying qualities of existing spaces and serving new programmatic needs.

A series of discussions between some of the founding instigators of the famous Manchester record label Factory were recently posted on YouTube. The conversations were recorded to celebrate 25 years since the opening of the label's infamous nightclub, the Haçienda, and the commemorative launch of a pair of trainers. Not training shoes, not footwear for organised sport or activity, but a bright and glaring pair of striped casual dance shoes, as worn by those who were/are part of the post-punk rave culture.

The Haçienda, which was once described as the world's best nightclub, predicted the need for the postindustrial society to populate the warehouse-type spaces that they were on the cusp of losing.

The industrial language of the Haçienda represented a massive shift in the sensibilities of a generation of club-goers. Before the 1980s, nightclubs did not exist; instead there were discos, which were glamorous, pretentious places with severe door policies that restricted entry to anybody not wearing the right clothes or footwear. The Haçienda, which was once described as the world's best nightclub, predicted the need for the postindustrial society to populate the warehouse-type spaces that they were on the cusp of losing.

Although the films were recorded at the studio of Ben Kelly, who designed the commemorative trainers, he is an almost silent character within the performance. While the rest of the group lean forwards, eager to share their anecdotes or insights into that strange and wonderful time, Kelly leans affably back from the table. Indeed, until video #4 of the set of nine, his contribution seems to be limited to ensuring that everyone has enough tea to drink and the whereabouts of the sugar. Only when the discussion is specifically about design does he really contribute. His direct prose is a welcome relief from the more florid and gossipy detailed explanations of his fellow conspirators. His description of the shoe is telling. He does not discuss the ironic or historical qualities of the design

or the appropriateness of it as a symbol of our postindustrial society. Nor does he mention that when the Haçienda opened it was probably the only club that would let anyone in who was wearing trainers. Instead he manages to sum up the whole design aesthetic as he carefully explains the choice of colours and the minutiae of the design, at one point actually bringing out one of the trainers that he had made earlier. He says: 'The main body of the trainer is the same colour as the club – pigeon blue ... the black and yellow stripes are synonymous with the club ... inevitably some orange ... different coloured eyelets and the laces could be striped.' And then, with affection for a small detail of a design that was constructed 25 years ago: 'I really wanted the graphic from the entrance to the club; a granite plaque with silver leaf, red enamel and the cedilla on the C.'[1]

Ben Kelly Design, The Haçienda, Manchester, 1982
The small and discreet plaque that signals the entrance. From the outside the club was hardly noticeable; little more than a factory-produced roller-shutter door.

Kelly does not engage in elaborate explanations of theories and ideas; he just has a clear and direct explanation of what was designed. Not since the late great James Stirling has a designer used so few words to convey so much. He is a designer who has a need to control every detail, almost obsessively. He is renowned for his response to the given and the exposure of the existing while inserting a totally new and appropriate layer of radical design. He is known for his passion for materials and for the manipulation of light.

The Ben Kelly Design (BKD) timeline of major projects is well documented. Projects from the early Howie store on the King's Road in London to the Manchester triumvirate of the

Ben Kelly Design, The Haçienda Trainers, June 2007
The trainers, designed to commemorate the 25th anniversary of the founding of the Haçienda in Manchester, are detailed to reflect the industrial quality of the legendary nightclub. The pigeon blue with hazard-warning details is reminiscent of the finishes in the club.

Ben Kelly Design, The Haçienda, Manchester, 1982
Traffic bollards signal the edge of the dance floor. These were 'found object▶ appropriated from the streets of Manchester, promoting a connection betwe▶ the post-punk, postindustrial generation and the warehouse-type space.

Haçienda (1982), Dry 201 (1989) and Factory Headquarters (1990) established him at the forefront of contemporary design. The list continues: Bar Ten in Glasgow (1991), the Basement Children's Gallery at the Science Museum (1995), followed by the Design Council Offices (1997), an apartment for Peter Saville (1996), Halfords Depots (1999), the Discovery Gallery in Walsall (2000), Borough Hotel, Edinburgh (2001) and the latter-day Gymbox projects (2003–06). BKD has worked through the usual spectrum of interior design project types: exhibition, offices, leisure, residential and retail. Throughout each project there are common themes including interesting relationships with clients, a thorough understanding of the nuances of the existing building, fastidious organisation with a real understanding of how people use spaces and, of course, materials. It is the assemblage of these appropriate, well thought-out finishes that generates a unique design language – off the peg to create bespoke identities.

The BKD office is situated next to Borough Market, which is underneath the main viaduct leading out of London Bridge Station. The studio is on the first floor of an adjacent market building and, as befits the most taciturn man in design, the office is accessed from a side street, through a discreet door

and up a dark staircase. However, once inside, just like Kelly▶ brain the studio is overflowing with drawings, materials, ide▶ and light. Initially the office appears chaotic – a wall of full-height windows dominates the room while the vast pile▶ of stacked samples, rolled plans, books and catalogues all jostle with little mementoes of travels. The lampshades real▶ are plastic buckets. A French hazard-sign warning of imminent electrocution is propped next to an orange shove▶ leaning against a folded-up ping-pong table. But there is an underlying order to the chaos – this office is built to be worked in. Things are close to hand. The chance arrangeme▶ of samples, products and objects provokes ideas. The underlying atmosphere of the space is workmanlike and unpretentious. It is obvious that Kelly is a man who needs to touch, to feel, to see, to sense the materials, finishes and products that he specifies.

In response to our opening discussion about the general perception of interiors practice and education, Kelly introduces himself as 'an old-fashioned interior designer'.[2] ▶ describes the subject as something that has integrity far beyond just surface consideration and he regards it as something that is 'very close to architecture, but it's not

The site-specific qualities of the existing building that can be teased out and repossessed in the transformation of a space are one of the major sources of atmosphere in his work.

Stacked piles of materials and samples litter the floor.

architecture', that actually has little to do with surface treatment, but has its basis in the manipulation and control of space. He explains that the starting point for any project is in the analysis and understanding of the unique qualities of the existing space, and suggests that there is a resonating element that springs from the original building that is crucial for the development of the project. This interpretive attitude can be traced back to the work of the well-known Italian interior architect Carlo Scarpa, although of course with vastly different visual results.

'When I get the plan then this is when the project begins. We sit around the table and discuss what it's telling us, what's possible, what can we keep and what has to go,' says Kelly. The site-specific qualities of the existing building that can be teased out and repossessed in the transformation of a space are one of the major sources of atmosphere in his work. It is from these readings that the process of organisation and assembly can begin. Kelly could be accused of not really doing very much; the basic spaces are relatively unaltered, many of the finishes are pre-existing and the new bits are very much the same as the old. He makes it look too easy. But that is exactly the point – he liberates the existing, not just in the way the space is exposed and manipulated, but also, and most importantly, the manner in which the new elements, insertions and materials echo the existing qualities.

The Basement Children's Gallery at the Science Museum in London exhibits these bare and uncovered characteristics.

Ben Kelly Design, Bar Ten, Glasgow, 1991
The interior was designed as the culmination of a journey that progresses from the busy shopping area, through a narrow alley and, finally, into the bar. Material selection and placement within the bar reinforce this narrative as they repeat and mimic materials found along the journey's path.

Ben Kelly Design, Dry 201, Manchester, 1989
The interior atmosphere animates the shop window of the bar in accordance with the desire to echo the Continental practice of maintaining a direct and open relationship between the interior space and the street.

BKD robustly stripped away much of the accumulated junk to reveal the bones of the space, the natural light and the structural finishes. The raw space was then quite simply organised with a new long, raked terrace floor that runs the length of the room, and animated by the deliberate and conscious application of materials. Brightly coloured surfaces are applied to embellish interesting features, which complement the exposed elements. The new elements emphasise the rawness; they use the same basic and crude language and yet are incredibly well thought-out and designed. The language is of a warehouse or factory for kids; it is totally suitable for children without being childish. The workings and mechanics of the place are (necessarily) revealed and relished; the electrical cables become decorative, the air-conditioning units are prominently displayed and even the lift panels are transparent. It is robust, truthful, unrefined and happy.

The work of the practice is often typecast as beginning and ending with a bold, varied and graphic palette of materials. But this underplays a crucial element of the work and Kelly should be given much greater credit for the careful and masterful planning of the spaces. Bar Ten in Glasgow has a European character. A large window on to the street makes it suitable for visiting during the day and at night, but once inside the space is very internally focused. A very crucial metre of transitional space at the entrance allows the visitor to mentally adjust to a new atmosphere.

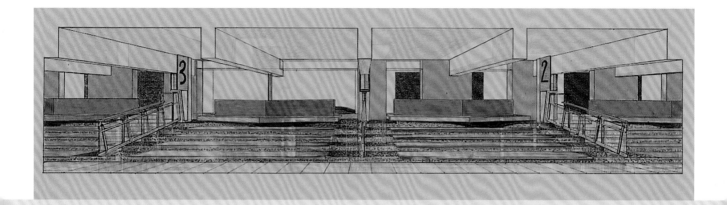

This focus on the movement of the entrance space also exists at Dry 201. Once again the big shop-window frames the activity within, thus creating a strong relationship with the street. But the visitor is once more moved into the darkness of the shadows at the side of the space to become accustomed to the enclosure and inward concentration of the room. As Kelly explains: 'I think it needed to be as public as it could be to the street, so people would be drawn into it, and also that kind of Continental bar, very open to the street. We wanted people to see in for sure.' This notion was reinforced and the memory of the previous furniture showroom was solidified through the reuse of an enormous plaster curtain. The detritus from an earlier existence was painted red and blatantly displayed in the shop window of the bar.

Within the Haçienda, now demolished, existed the most theatrical architectural promenade. The presence of the club on the street was almost nonexistent. The clubber would pass through a small dark door into a tight lobby, from there into a slightly larger area and 'then into a massive cathedral-like space which heightened and magnified the experience, you became overwhelmed once you were in there, it took you over'. This is typical of BKD's work, where the movement is linear and spaces are designed in series, as a progression of scenes for the user to inhabit, each connected to the last through the themed use of materials, textures and colours, but each with a distinct and identifiable atmosphere.

In all of Ben Kelly's work, the atmospheric condition of each project is born out of a mixture of the pragmatic use of the qualities of the existing space, the planning and organisation of the new function, and the fabrication of an identity through the creative use of specific materials. He enjoys the conversation between new and old, the act of bringing life to the redundant, the process of remembering, of revealing and of constructing a new contemporary layer of meaning and animation. ∆

Notes
1. www.youtube.com/watch?v=evaCQLEuZQs&mode=related&search=
2. In conversation with the authors.

Ben Kelly Design, The Basement, National Museum of Science and Industry, London, 1995
Kelly envisioned this part of the museum as fluid and colourful. It was conceived as a series of interconnected spaces that encourage children to relax and be creative.

The designers have transformed the space into a stimulating place for children to investigate. The new and the existing materials are raw and robust, and the applied finishes are as tough as the stripped-down space.

Living with Freud

Lilian Chee introduces several art installations displayed at the Freud Museum in north London. While each individually opens up further critique of Freud's practice and its cultural impact, collectively they measure the ability of objects to charge interior atmospheres with provocations of gender, modernity, ethnicity, objectivity and domesticity.

Susan Hiller, *At the Freud Museum*, 1994
Installation view of a vitrine made as part of 'The Reading Room' project, commissioned by Book Works, London, which featured artists and writers in Glasgow, London and Oxford from March to May 1994.

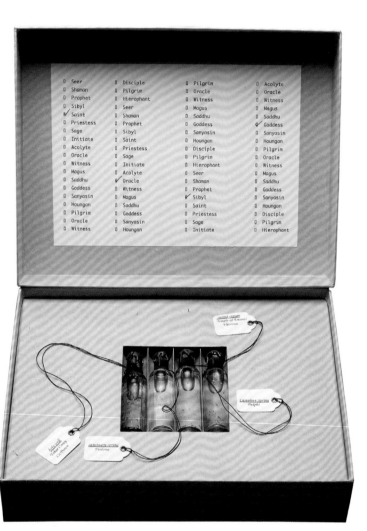

Susan Hiller, 'Sophia/Wisdom', *From the Freud Museum*, 1993
Prototype of a box containing waters collected at sacred sites in corked and sealed antique bottles. The prototype was later developed for Hiller's installation *At the Freud Museum* in 1994.

Sophie Calle, 'The Wedding Dress', *Appointment with Sigmund Freud*, 199 Curated by James Putnam, *Appointment with Sigmund Freud* displayed relic from Calle's own life among Freud's possessions.

Once the home and office of psychoanalyst Sigmund Freud, London's Freud Museum is a well-preserved collection that entices both the curious and the converted into its rooms. Here, the manner in which Freud's objects give enduring meaning to his spaces needs reiteration. Notably, the spatial framework for such objects, which include key pieces of furniture and antique figurines, has been painstakingly re-enacted; initially following Freud's move from Vienna, and subsequently, over time, by the present museum and its curators.

It is therefore unusual that the museum has enabled contemporary artists to reoccupy and reinterpret an almost sacred context through the provocative medium of installation art. These artistic interventions use Freudian-inspired objects as controversial levers to simultaneously affirm, challenge or complicate the interior's historical and cultural meanings.

Susan Hiller's *At the Freud Museum* (1994) comprised 22 brown, custom-made archaeological boxes, each containing : found or collected object, its pictorial representation, a text and a label. The work religiously encased 'beautiful, utilitaria tedious, scholarly, macabre, rare, banal, eerie, and sentimenta objects' in nondescriptive, miniature boxed interiors that Hill doubly confined within an existing glass vitrine in Freud's bedroom.[1] The contents of the boxes, such as cow-shaped mi jugs, water from sacred sites sealed in antique bottles, a Ouij board, instruments and instructions for dowsing, and a Punch-and-Judy comedy scene, are all familiar in that they allude to Freud's possessions and his unusual collection of myths, jokes and dreams. Yet Hiller's boxed objects do not merely copy what is there. They raise abrasive views about gender, modernity, ethnicity, objectivity and domesticity.

The work religiously encased 'beautiful, utilitarian, tedious, scholarly, macabre, rare, banal, eerie, and sentimental objects' in nondescriptive, miniature boxed interiors that Hiller doubly confined within an existing glass vitrine in Freud's bedroom.

Sarah Lucas, *Hysterical Attack (Mouths and Eyes)*, 1999, in
Beyond the Pleasure Principle, 2000
Also curated by James Putnam, this installation view shows the chair
in Freud's study. In the background, above Freud's couch, is Lucas'
'Prière de Toucher', a large photograph of the artist's torso.

They are deeply unsettling because they manifest underlying questions of truth, fiction and mortality operating within a specific interior milieu that Hiller calls 'the Father's house'.

The box as a device for entering the Freudian milieu is important. It frames the objects within; that is, it gives the objects coherence and legitimacy. Perhaps not coincidentally, the scene of psychoanalysis is also commonly referred to as a 'frame' regulating duration, cost and spatial arrangement of the psychoanalytic experience. As we attempt to decipher Hiller's objects through the double enclosures of the glass vitrine and cardboard box, we become conscious of the museum's interior frame – its boundaries, highlights, stories and routes – and of how this frame conditions our vision and the visuality of Freud's practice and spaces. Working through association, memory, fantasy, dreamlike states and, most importantly, narrative, we encounter the Freud Museum within Hiller's box-set museum as a series of episodic inventions, whose frame of reference remains, at best, tenuous and imaginative.

As the proverbial site of the talking cure, Freud's couch is a psychoanalytic icon. The shape of the couch also recalls the vulnerable, reclining body of the analysand. In Sophie Calle's *Appointment with Sigmund Freud* (1999), a silk wedding dress is draped suggestively over the couch. The wedding dress is a garment linked to purity and virginity, and to a woman's sexual coming-of-age. It is hauntingly also the last article of clothing a woman chooses to be dressed in for burial. Calle recasts the Father's house as a repressed feminine space, whose foundations and knowledge are, in part, nurtured by frequently unnamed female patients who collaboratively constructed the discipline with their confessions and stories. Instead of perpetuating the stereotype of the female hysteric,

Calle's choice of dress raises the problem of the female body as the object of consumption and derision. As the silk dress lies limp on the couch, it accentuates a complex memory of forgotten sitters – Bertha P, Anna O, Irma and Dora – whose identities are intricately bound to the father figure.

A different anthropomorphic memory is suggested in Sarah Lucas' *Hysterical Attack* (*Mouths and Eyes*) (1999), where papier-mâché, tentacle-like and faintly feminine splayed tights-as-limbs sprout out of cheap, second-hand shop chairs. Lucas has wittily covered the chairs and their abject prostheses in magazine cutouts featuring either mouths or eyes, thus gesturing the importance of oral and scopic registers in Freudian sexual theories. More importantly, the chairs remember the bodies in this room as sexed – male, female; psychoanalyst, patient – and the power to see, be seen, to speak, or be spoken to as inherently gendered capacities within this plush space.

These artistic interventions enable us to negotiate the frame of Freud's house by radically transforming our perception and encounter. Through them, these interiors embody our presence as much as they remember Freud's past. ⚙

The author thanks the artists, James Putnam, Book Works and the Freud Museum for their assistance and generosity.

Note
1. Susan Hiller, *After the Freud Museum*, Book Works (London), 2000, unpaginated.

Spatial Hardware

In light of his visit in 2007 to the Documenta 12 art institution in Kassel, Germany, **Rochus Urban Hinkel** speculates on the reciprocity of 'spatial hardware' and 'spatial software' to create interior atmosphere. This essay traverses between the two as he takes us through the exhibition spaces housed in the temporary urban and industrial 'gallery' environment, Aue Pavilion.

Jean Baudrillard speculates in *The System of Objects* that where design is about the calculation of function, atmosphere is created through the manipulation of materials, forms and spaces. More importantly, atmosphere is the 'systematic cultural connotation at the level of objects'.[1] Objects and surfaces, form and light, material and colour are often described as the ingredients for the design of the interior. They are used to construct space, its functions and appearance. But how strong is their contribution towards the creation of an atmosphere? The temporal, ephemeral, intangible elements and sensations within interiors, together with cultural connotations, preconceived knowledge and personal memories, also factor in the formation of interior atmosphere. Often described as phenomenological, these influences attend to the experience of a perceiving subject open to a world of sensations. I call such atmospheric influences, 'spatial software' – a term more inclusive than the predetermined phenomenological definition with its assumptions about the fixity of the perceiving subject. If there is 'spatial software', then we can presume there also must be 'spatial hardware', which pertains to what can be measured – the construction of the interior, the definition of boundaries, materials and details. Spatial software and spatial hardware are co-dependent and co-present; one does not mean much without the other, though their proportions vary depending on the specific interior under consideration.

I am at Documenta, an ephemeral contemporary art institution that is held as a quinquennial event. Inaugurated in 1955 as an addition to a federal garden show, it has taken over the German town of Kassel for the twelfth time. This year, a temporary greenhouse, the Aue Pavilion, appears prominently positioned on a field of grass in the Karlsaue Park opposite the baroque Orangerie. The artistic director of Documenta 12, Roger M Buergel, explains that the Aue Pavilion is a contemporary orangerie, not for housing exotic plants, but for protecting instead the symbolic value of art. The French architects of the original Aue Pavilion concept, Anne Lacaton and Jean-Philippe Vassal, supply what is necessary for Documenta – more space. The Aue Pavilion is distinctive for its use of banal and industrial materials and details and its lack of pretension. A simple steel-post construction meets a rudimentary red bitumen floor, and the walls are clad in ribbed polycarbonate sheeting. This deployment of readily available materials and rudimentary details facilitates the inexpensive provision of a large volume. The pavilion's industrial appearance, as a counterpoint to the baroque ornamentation of the original Orangerie, plays with preconceived ideas of the greenhouse type and its association with suburban garden centres.

Placed in the context of Documenta, the 'greenhouse' is necessarily recontextualised as unexpected accommodation for a contemporary art exhibition.

Placed in the context of Documenta, the 'greenhouse' is necessarily recontextualised as unexpected accommodation for a contemporary art exhibition. Furthermore, the historical and cultural context that is Documenta contributes to the spatial software that shapes the atmosphere of the Aue Pavilion. It must be remembered that the Aue Pavilion sits in relation to a series of other exhibition venues all dedicated to the Documenta event, manifesting an atmosphere of festivity in Kassel for the period of a hundred days and nights.

and Software

Aue Pavilion, Documenta 12, Kassel, Germany, 2007
Documenta's temporary Aue Pavilion was situated in the Karlsaue
Park opposite the historical Orangerie. The Orangerie was built in
1711 by the architect Hofbaumeister Johann Conrad Giesler and was
once a summer residence for the landgrave Karl.

The interior is reminiscent of an arbour-like, shady garden alcove;
where trees or climbing plants might be expected there are instead
diaphanous curtains that obscure the light through layers.

Buergel and his partner Ruth Noack, the curator of Documenta, write in the preface of the exhibition catalogue that 'the big exhibition has no form. More often than not exhibitions come with a theme or are dedicated to a particular artist, a certain era or style, however Documenta's inherent formlessness contradicts any such approach.' [2] Instead, three leitmotifs framed as questions open up a forum for debate: 'Is Modernity our Antiquity?'; 'What is bare life?'; and 'Education! What has to be done?'. Buergel and Noack avoid placing art in a curated field of meanings and interpretations. Instead, the work of the collected artists is meant to speak for itself in direct dialogue with the visitors who attend Documenta. The unobtrusive architecture of the Aue Pavilion facilitates this meeting place between art and visitor. Monumental gestures and novel formal expression, otherwise deployed to articulate an exclusive status for the art-object in the world of art markets or 'high culture', have been avoided. The pavilion opens itself to encounter, and in terms of its architectural signs, demands little of the visitor except for an attention to the experience at hand.

Buergel critiques the contemporary art industry for manufacturing art that is detached from its viewers and its tendency to operate as spectacle and entertainment. He questions existing exhibition practice and places the encounter between art and the viewer in the centre of his

Artworks are loosely composed in no apparent hierarchy about this spacious interior. (Artwork: Alice Creischer, *Mach doch heute Lobby*, 1998–2007.)

The interior is modulated by different intensities of natural and artificial light. Translucent wall panels form the physical and visual boundary between interior and exterior.

Discreet steel-profile posts, set in a regular rhythm, are the only visible structural elements and plunge directly into the dirt-red bitumen floor. (Artwork: Gerwald Rockenschaub, *Klassenzimmer*, 2007.)

aspirations for Documenta 12. This encounter is framed by interior space, and contributes to the concept of spatial atmosphere that I am forwarding here. As the Aue Pavilion was the only new building constructed for Documenta 12, it becomes the spatial articulation of Buergel's vision for potential encounters between art and audience, which, in turn, put questions of representation and interpretation aside. The pavilion could be seen as an anti-museum in that it offers an invitation to open dialogue and uninhibited engagement. In what way does this influence the interior atmosphere and the spatial experience?

On the interior of the pavilion the spatial hardware, all the material and structural signs of architecture, almost disappear. The spatial hardware is not interested in fine detail or expensive material; its task is to enclose an expansive volume given over to display and the possibility of different forms of encounter. The interior creates spaces of potential in which audience members can become participants in the curation and interpretation of art as they forge their own path between one cluster of work and another. In one sense the atmosphere created in the Aue Pavilion is not ready-made, but created in the midst of the milling people who gather to experience the art; it emerges where the interior, the audience and the art come together simultaneously.

An analytical reading of the spatial hardware of the temporary pavilion quickly gives way to a more experiential

apprehension of spatial software and how atmosphere is aroused between these two registers. There are subtle distinctions. For instance, the distribution of ancient Chinese chairs throughout the pavilion, a contribution by the Chinese artist Ai Weiweis, seems to rest between the art, the architecture and the spatial experience, offering respite as a place to rest. The chairs form small circles suitable for groups of up to 20 people – an interior within the interior. As a gathering spot for guided tours, participants, even strangers, are encouraged to exchange their experiences and thoughts. There is empty space, where no art is evident, with empty walls. The exterior skin and its interior curtained counterpart only offer enclosure, never a surface to exhibit or hang art. The art sits away from the pavilion's skin.

While the first impression of the pavilion's interior is of a massive, endlessly open space punctuated by loosely placed art, eventually the space narrows and I cross a threshold that offers a visual connection to the outside. A sonic experience, part of an art installation, also marks this transition. In the next part of the pavilion, partitions are more dominant and begin to organise a constant spatial flux between walls with art and empty walls. Relations between artworks are set up in multiple ways. Enclosed for a while I forget the outside again, until a huge picture window reveals the baroque Orangerie. I am almost at the end of my progression through the Aue Pavilion. The open spaces inside the pavilion operate as an

Towards the deeper recesses of the greenhouse, the light darkens and artificial lights focused on points of attention augment the space; the exterior recedes further, becoming increasingly muffled.

Despite the architects' original intention, the greenhouse that is the Aue Pavilion is an internalised, sealed and fully air-conditioned space. This was part of Anne Lacaton's and Jean Philippe Vassal's dispute with Documenta 12. They subsequently retracted their involvement before the Aue Pavilion was completed.

At the end of the journey through the interior of the Aue Pavilion, the view opens up to the outside and the historic Orangerie.

urban interior, similar to a public space or sphere, only enclosed. Smaller passages open up on to larger public squares, large art objects take me by surprise, and then smaller delights can be discovered around corners. Classes of chattering excitable schoolchildren pass by. Not afraid of running around or talking loudly, they too appear to be promenading a town square or boulevard. The pavilion creates a spatial envelope of peculiar humility, offering a social space in which everyone can perform a part in response to contemporary art.

As it is a hot summer's day in Kassel, the climatised interior is well tempered; it is a pleasant place to be. The experience also benefits from the intense sunlight in July. A strong relation to natural light at certain junctures in the pavilion would transform when it is dark or raining outside, or simply overcast. These qualities, facilitated through the ephemera of spatial software, make this interior a space where the experienced atmosphere constantly shifts, presenting different experiences for different visitors. The ephemeral qualities of the pavilion combine with the intellectual concepts behind the pavilion. The pavilion's spatial software achieves an unexpected affect on many of its visitors. Even if the pavilion does not convince everyone, it creates awareness of the role the interior plays in our experience of art. Though the spatial hardware, in the opinion of the architects, Lacaton and Vassal, has failed, success of another kind has been achieved. Though they were not happy that the pavilion had to become a hermetically sealed environment controlled by ungainly air-conditioning units visible on an approach from

Karlsaue Park, nevertheless the interior creates the potential for different experiences aroused in contact with the art.

Through the mingling of spatial software and spatial hardware, the failures and successes of the Aue Pavilion contribute towards an interior atmosphere. Time filters the residue of atmospheric effects so that some impressions remain more vivid in my mind, while others fade. Memory, prior experience and knowledge of the serial Documenta events, discussions with others, even photography as an augmentation to memory and experience, continue to develop further layers to the interior atmosphere of the Aue Pavilion, even once I have left Kassel far behind. Atmosphere is a contemporary experience in real time, but it is also composed of the residual memories of our past presence in an interior. And importantly atmosphere is an ongoing process of negotiation between the experienced, the remembered, the thought, the known, the analysed, the imagined as well as the forgotten. Atmosphere manifests as an ongoing state of flux, and that is what makes it so hard to grasp. It is not simply a singular moment of sensory apprehension; it is an ongoing relation to an interior that opens up a constant development and reiteration of unfolding experience. ⧊

Notes
1. Jean Baudrillard, *The System of Objects*, trans James Benedict, Verso (London, New York), 2005, p 49.
2. Roger M Buergel and Ruth Noack, 'Preface', *Documenta 12 Catalogue*, Taschen (Kassel), 2007, p 11.

The Atmosphere of Interior Urbanism

OMA at IIT

Office for Metropolitan Architecture (OMA), McCormick Tribune Campus Centre, Illinois Institute of Technology (IIT), Chicago, 1997–2003
Mies is recaptured through OMA's atmospheric lens. In the same way that weather has become a subject of installation art, atmosphere has become the subject of architecture's material and spatial effects.

Charles Rice explores interior atmosphere in a site challenged by existing infrastructure among a generally deteriorating urban scene. Crediting the Office for Metropolitan Architecture's IIT building in Chicago with refiguring the field via the deployment of complex spatial planning, integration of the building with the elevated train rail and a highly differentiated illumination scheme, he ultimately defines the nature of interior urbanism, an urbanity and atmosphere beyond the limits of the building envelope.

Mies van der Rohe's campus at the Illinois Institute of Technology presents an ambivalent urban condition. It is often seen as the epitome of the Modernist tabula rasa approach to planning: the obliteration of context and the imposition of a new and alienating order. Yet his campus pla can be understood in terms of the larger, socially and politically engaged efforts at reforming Chicago's Near South Side. In this context, Mies' plan has been seen as a 'figured field', an inclusive and energised condition of urban linkage. It is undeniable, however, that in recent times IIT as an institution has suffered from falling enrolments, and the campus has developed a reputation as an unsafe environmen

OMA's McCormick Tribune Campus Centre (1997–2003) finds its *raison d'être* in this complex situation. OMA responds to Mies' campus with an interior urbanism, an arrangement of diverse programmes in a condition that heightens the sense of their relationality. These programmes are a mix of academic and leisure facilities that cater to a range of different users at different times of the day, week and year.

The building casts its glow outwards on to the campus. Illumination and differentiation occur through the effects of material. Programmatic differentiation becomes atmospheric differentiation.

The way they are disposed within the centre relates to the pathways and crossing points that connect functions in the wider campus structure. In this way, the Campus Centre is an intensification of the experience of the grid; the building's organisation embraces the wider campus conditions from the start.

One of the building's most surprising aspects is the way in which it literally incorporates the elevated railway line into its fabric. Where such a piece of infrastructure might be seen to be an impediment to the development of such a building – and, indeed, a major impediment to the integration and therefore the urbanisation of the campus itself – OMA capitalises on it for the way it contributes to an atmosphere of the urban within the building. The shell surrounding the elevated train insulates the building against noise from the railway, making building on this site possible. Yet the incorporation of the shell within the building, and the palpable vibration of the trains passing overhead, means that the trajectory of the train and its urban rhythm is also made

present within the building. This is another way of describing the building's interior urbanism: the train is not engaged with as it would be in the city. It is not a literal presence above a city street. However, its atmospheric presence within the building heightens the effect of the building's interiority. If one might say that cities have atmosphere through the combination of large-scale and often contingent variables – the width of streets, the scale of blocks, topography, zoning – then interior urbanism has atmosphere as the result of deliberate architectural effects. It is the architectural organisation that makes the presence of the train part of the urban atmosphere of the building.

Given the organisation of the building in terms of trajectories across the campus, the programmes it incorporates are encountered almost in a glancing fashion. One does not head directly towards a particular function or service. Rather, one comes to a point or crossing, a moment of intensity, where options become available. Changes in the floor level mean that the main entry track becomes a bridge

Space itself is montaged. Programmatic zones are spliced together, producing abrupt linkages and opportunistic appropriations.

The building slides underneath the elevated railway's sound-absorbing tube.

Interior surfaces enfold exterior conditions through reflection. The building produces its double. At the same time, different zones are defined through light modulations, which are effects of material surfaces.

that allows one to survey a range of activities at the centre of the building. Varying levels of illumination, and contrast between light and dark zones, ensure that this field of possibilities is variegated in a way that occludes certain areas, depending on position and viewpoint, and also creates an attraction to others. One has to keep moving in order for the full range of functions and services to be revealed. Along the way, incidental pockets of space and activity become defined, sometimes by the presence of furniture, sometimes by the height of a ceiling or a change in floor surface.

Illumination and differentiation happen as much by materials as by lighting effects. Orange polycarbonate cladding becomes a filter of light into the building, producing zones flooded with orange light at particular points. The counterpoint green drywall used for the ceilings, and deliberately left in a raw state, offers a literal balance to the intensity of the orange, as if trying to cancel the effect of afterimages. This atmospheric sense of colour and light produces an interior condition differentiated diurnally as well as spatially. Some areas appear in twilight, others in an even daylight, and yet others in a kind of nocturnal glow. An urban

touring of the building's programmes is also a temporal one: one accelerates through a day of activities, across various seasons, into various time zones.

In the same way that weather has become a subject of installation art – OMA's orange glow bears comparison to Olafur Eliasson's *Weather project* installation at Tate Modern in 2004 – atmosphere has become the subject of architecture's material and spatial effects. This is not, however, a concern with the atmosphere and the effect of weather on a building's exterior fabric, and the consequent celebration of joints, details and materials that would mark the presence of these effects over time.[2] Rather, weather has become an interior condition in order that a building might produce an urbanism – and an urbanity – beyond its boundaries. △

Notes
1. See Sarah Whiting, 'Bas-relief urbanism: Chicago's figured field', in Phyllis Lambert (ed), *Mies in America*, Harry N Abrams (New York), 2001, pp 642–91.
2. See Mohsen Mostafavi and David Leatherbarrow, *On Weathering: The Life of Buildings in Time*, MIT Press (Cambridge, MA and London), 1993.

Artists of the Floating World

SANAA, Niedermayr and the Construction of Atmosphere

Hugh Campbell expands upon the mutually collaborative spatial qualities evoked in the photographic works of Walter Niedermayr and the architecture of Kazuyo Sejima and Ryue Nishizawa of Tokyo-based practice SANAA. Describing their relation as forming a 'thickened presence', he alludes to a particular atmosphere reliant on an ambiguity of scale, detail and discernible proximity that serves to liberate the architecture and the photographs from mere documentation whereby instead they figure as transparent recordings of spatial intentions.

Top: Walter Niedermayr, Bildraum S 1, 2002 (Ryue Nishizawa, Takeo Head Office, Tokyo, 2000): diptych, each 126 x 103 cm
In one of his first photographs of SANAA's work, Niedermayr adjusts the exposure so that people appear to float without anchorage in a white-out world.

Bottom: Walter Niedermayr, Bildraum S 152, 2006 (SANAA, Glass Pavilion at the Toledo Museum of Art, 2006): diptych, each 126 x 103 cm
The curving walls of the Glass Pavilion produce a complex play of transparency and reflectivity.

Since the earliest years of photography, architecture has been one of its favourite subjects. Static, modelled by light and most often rectilinear, buildings lent themselves to the nascent techniques and aesthetics of the new medium. More recently, architecture has become central to the practice of many photographers. From Candida Höfer's sober depictions of hushed, emptied rooms and Hiroshi Sugimoto's blurred images of iconic Modernist buildings to Thomas Demand's photographs of meticulously constructed models, built space finds itself being thoroughly examined and reinvented through the camera lens.

The photographs of the architecture of SANAA taken by Walter Niedermayr over the past six years form an interesting addition to this emerging field. The work has recently been the subject of an exhibition curated by deSingel in Antwerp and an accompanying publication. The photographs take the form of large-scale diptychs. Although there are some exterior views, most of the diptychs depict the interior spaces of buildings including the Toledo Glass Pavilion, Ohio (2006), the Naoshima Ferry Terminal in Kagawa, Japan (2006) and the Zollverein School of Management and Design, Essen, Germany (2006). They seem to capture perfectly the pallid, ethereal atmospheres that characterise the work of Sejima and Nishizawa. They also clearly represent a continuation of the themes and visual language established in Niedermayr's own earlier work. The Sud-Tirolean photographer is best known for his spectacular serial images of snowy Alpine landscapes sparsely populated by brightly clad skiers and climbers. These figures are tiny in scale and yet remain distinctly visible against the vast expanses of whiteness in which they appear to float without anchorage. The lack of familiar cues of scale and distance confers a kind of liberation on the figures, and because they appear in

sequences of images they become more than anonymous, interchangeable motifs, gradually becoming distinguishable by the details of their clothing and by the groupings they form. Rather than seeming blank and inhospitable, the snow-covered mountains are rendered strangely domestic.

In SANAA's buildings, Niedermayr appears to have found an interior landscape with something of the same character and effect. Clearly the architects also sensed that the photographer might respond to their work, as they explain: 'Someone at SANAA saw Niedermayr's work in a gallery and we invited Walter to come and do his work at the 21st Century Museum of Contemporary Art, Kanazawa. ... SANAA loved the work. Niedermayr also loved the work so he continued to visit our projects on his own time and has done

While the photographs could never be thought of as a straightforward documentation of the buildings, they do manage vividly to describe what it might be like to inhabit these spaces.

so ever since.'[1] While agreeing that they share an aesthetic sensibility 'in the best way', the architects are keen to stress that they have little input into the photographic process and that the photographs 'are very much independent viewpoints, as much about Niedermayr as about our architecture'.

While the photographs could never be thought of as a straightforward documentation of the buildings, they do manage vividly to describe what it might be like to inhabit these spaces. The horizon line that bifurcates many of the views serves to draw us into the images while also

Walter Niedermayr, Bildraum S 131, 2006 (SANAA, Zollverein School of Management and Design, Essen, Germany, 2006): diptych, each 126 x 103 cm
Niedermayr's photograph highlights how the scattering of large openings across the thin facade of the Zollverein institute lends a fragile delicacy to the interior.

View of exhibition 'Kazuyo Sejima + Ryue Nishizawa/SANAA & Walter Niedermayr', deSingel international art campus, Antwerp, Belgium, 2007
The lighting and furnishing were designed by SANAA to extend the mood of the images into the exhibition space.

establishing an equivalence between top and bottom so that gravity seems strangely absent. Like those tiny figures traversing the Alps, people appear to float between evanescent layers of whiteness and transparency. As Niedermayr explains: 'Nothing in the image should dominate, so that all the elements have the same valence and visibility, from people to objects and architectural structures.'[2] Once again, there are few clues of scale and orientation, just an all-pervasive atmosphere, which even the red fire extinguisher visible in the corner of the main hall of the Zollverein School of Management and Design cannot dispel (it might even be said to heighten it). These feel like spaces in which one is immersed rather than inserted.

In an interview that predates his collaboration with SANAA, Niedermayr stressed that he was primarily interested in representing the experience of space. Most obviously, his use of the diptych offers a stereoscopic, rather than a monocular view. But in fact Niedermayr makes multiple technical adjustments at every stage of the photographic process – prolonging exposure times, using strong filters, lightening the print during development, reducing colour densities while enlarging the images – all in the service of trying to get closer to the essential spatial experience. He explains: 'The most exciting moment is always when you are perceiving the space with all of your senses and the image, or the idea of the image, takes shape in your mind. Then comes the making of the picture ... This experience of space has nothing to do with architecture. An architect would probably have no interest in my images as documents of his or her work.'[3] But while they may not function as documents, for SANAA his photographs certainly seem to get back to the underlying 'idea' of the architecture, to the initial dream of what the spaces might be like: 'Sometimes we are surprised by the images in that they get to something that is very much

our work but not before seen by us,' explains Nishizawa. 'Again, they are their own viewpoint. But because we share a sensibility the photograph always has some strong connection to the "purest" intentions of the work.'

As works like John Szarkowski's classic *The Idea of Louis Sullivan* (1956) demonstrate, photographs of buildings can do far more than record: they can reveal an architecture's motivating ideas. 'In the most general sense photography makes architecture,' comment SANAA. 'A building starts out with a thousand views but in the end one, maybe two, views get taken. In many ways that becomes the building.' At its most straightforward, this may be taken to mean that the photo provides the iconic image of a project. Beyond this there is the possibility that photograph and building are equivalent in some more thoroughgoing way. Certainly one can begin to find parallels between the formality, delicacy and consistency of tone in Niedermayr's diptychs, and those very same qualities in SANAA's work. Far from being 'transparent' records, the photographs are evidently deliberate, artful constructs. The even, diffuse light that SANAA seem to favour in their interiors and which they produce through the manipulation of surface and skin, is then reproduced by different means by Niedermayr. Equally, the feeling of uninterrupted volume, which SANAA produce through the suppression of structure and the attenuation of thicknesses, is then reproduced by Niedermayr's undifferentiated depth of field. From one medium to the other the means change, but the ends remain the same.

This rich mutuality suggests that photography, rather than marking the completion of a piece of architecture through the recording of a building's pristine spaces before they are sullied by occupation, can become more integral to the design process itself. Nowadays the ubiquity of Photoshop and other software means that 'realistic' interiors and exteriors can be depicted even at the earliest stages of a design. But the

Walter Niedermayr, Bildraum S 154, 2006 (SANAA, Glass Pavilion at the Toledo Museum of Art, Ohio, 2006): diptych, each 103 x 126 cm
In Niedermayr's treatment of the Toledo Glass Pavilion, people again appear to float, although here the interior offers more spatial and material variety, reflected in the photographs' extended depth of field.

Walter Niedermayr, Bildraum S 105, 2006 (SANAA, Novartis Campus WSJ-158, Basel, Switzerland, 2006): diptych, each 103 x 126 cm
In the Novartis Campus, a seamless continuity is established between interior and exterior. Niedermayr's image emphasises the slenderness of the structure and the resultant expansiveness of the glazing.

photographic process can also be used in more imaginative ways. SANAA themselves often use photographs of models to advance their designs, by immediately suggesting the nature and character of the volumes. Of course scale models cannot precisely reproduce spatial conditions at full scale – the ratio of air and light to the thickness of enclosing materials and the size of openings is different. This accounts for the slight air of unreality evident in the work of contemporary photographers who work with models: Thomas Demand, Oliver Boberg and

James Casebere, for instance. But it may also account for the peculiar interior atmospheres of SANAA's buildings which, with their pervasive whiteness, their slender bones and flimsy surfaces can often feel more like models than real places: this is particularly evident in Sejima's House in Plum Grove, Tokyo (2003), its thin steel walls looking for all the world like cardboard cutouts. The slight naivety inherent in a snapshot of a hasty model becomes a precise quality to be aimed for in the detailed construction. And it is this quality that Niedermayr's photographs subsequently rediscover.

Everything seems suspended within these spaces. They produce a kind of 'thick present', a slice of space in which time itself is stilled so that, just as the photographs share qualities with the architecture, the architecture also begins to feel like a photograph. Hitherto, the collaboration between SANAA and Niedermayr has followed a set pattern: they design and construct buildings, which he subsequently photographs. But it is interesting to consider what both parties might gain from a more complete intertwining of their respective artistic processes – a constructive and a depictive medium in pursuit of a shared spatial language. ᴆ

Notes
1. All quotes from SANAA from an email interview conducted by the author in July 2007.
2. Marion Piffer Damiani in conversation with Walter Niedermayr, in Walter Niedermayr, *Civil Operations*, Hatje Cantz, 2003, pp 160–62.
3. Ibid, p 161.

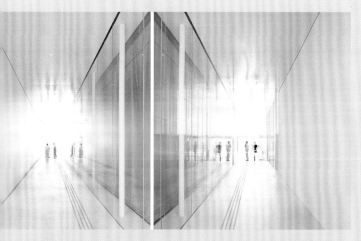

Walter Niedermayr, Bildraum S 3, 2004 (SANAA, 21st Century Museum of Contemporary Art, Kanazawa, Ishikawa, Japan, 2004): diptych, each 126 x 103 cm
According to the architects, these are the first photographs by Niedermayr of their work that they encountered. The diptych format draws attention to the consistent character of SANAA's spaces: no matter how they are approached or from where they are seen, they retain a recognisable atmosphere.

Contributors

Mary Anne Beecher is an associate professor in the Department of Architecture at the University of Oregon. She teaches in the interior architecture programme and specialises in the history of interiors and furniture. She publishes on topics related to the history of the American vernacular interior, the history of the interior design profession and design history pedagogy. She received her PhD in American Studies from the University of Iowa and is currently completing a book manuscript on the history of American domestic storage.

Graeme Brooker is the programme leader of the undergraduate and postgraduate interior design courses at the Manchester Metropolitan University, and is the director of IE-Interior Educators. **Sally Stone** is the director of the College of Continuity in Architecture at the Manchester School of Architecture. They have written extensively together on interiors, including: *Re-readings: Interior Architecture and the Design Principles of Remodelling Existing Buildings* (RIBA Enterprises, 2004), *Form and Structure: The Organisation of Interior Space* (AVA, 2007), and the forthcoming *From Organisation to Decoration: A Routledge Reader of Interiors*.

Hugh Campbell is a senior lecturer in architecture at University College Dublin where he teaches design and history and theory of architecture and is coordinator of the graduate course. He has published widely and has lectured and taught at many universities worldwide. His areas of research include Irish architecture and urbanism; the representation of space in photography and other media; space in postwar Europe; and the relationship between the construction of the self and the construction of space, a subject on which he is currently completing a book entitled *In Here and Out There*.

Rachel Carley completed her PhD in architecture in 2006. Her thesis, 'Whiteread's Soundings of Architecture', moulds a series of contours between the British artist Rachel Whiteread's sculptures and architectural discourse. Soundings are taken in order to explore the complex ways in which the artist enlists architectural drawing and modelling practices to shed light on the rich interior lives of quotidian spaces and typological structures frequently overlooked. Since 1994, she has also been designing slip cast, earthenware ceramics that have been widely published in New Zealand design magazines. She is currently the programme coordinator of the Interior Architecture Department at Unitec in Auckland, New Zealand.

Lilian Chee is an architectural designer, writer and architectural theorist. She was trained at the Bartlett School of Architecture in London and at the National University of Singapore, where she currently teaches. She has researched and published on architectural subjectivity, gendered spaces and questions of domesticity. Her previous works include a study of poet Sylvia Plath's London house and an investigation of the Raffles Hotel in Singapore through its floral and animal associations.

Hélène Frichot is a senior lecturer in the Program of Architecture, RMIT, Melbourne, Australia. While architecture is her first discipline, she also holds a PhD in philosophy from the University of Sydney. Her work is published broadly in scholarly journals and books, as well as in professional art and design journals. With Esther Anatolitis she co-curates the Architecture + Philosophy Public Lecture Series (www.architecturephilosophy.rmit.edu.au).

Rochus Urban Hinkel is a practising architect, academic and curator. His work ranges from small-scale furniture to urban design schemes, he has won a number of awards and has been published and exhibited in Europe, Asia and Australia. His research and practice investigates concepts of spatial performance and experience as a nexus between architecture, interior and the urban sphere. He is a founding member of the interdisciplinary research group Urban Interior in the School of Architecture and Design at RMIT.

Paul James teaches in the Architecture School at Victoria University of Wellington, New Zealand. His essay in this issue is part of a larger study in which he considers the role of images within philosophies of history.

Ted Krueger is the Associate Dean of Architecture and an associate professor in the School of Architecture at Rensselaer Polytechnic Institute, where he is a director of the PhD programme in the architectural sciences. His research focuses on human–environment interaction, and the technological augmentation of human perception. He has lectured, exhibited and published on an international basis for 20 years.

Founded in 1997 by **Paul Lewis**, **Marc Tsurumaki** and **David J Lewis**, Lewis.Tsurumaki.Lewis (LTL Architects) is an architecture and design partnership that explores the intersection between theory and practice. The New York-based firm has completed academic, institutional, retail and restaurant projects throughout the US. It received the 2007 Cooper-Hewitt National Design Award for Interior Architecture and represented the US in the US Pavilion at the 2004 Venice Architecture Biennale. Publications include *Opportunistic Architecture* (2008) and *Situation Normal... Pamphlet Architecture #21* (1998). Paul Lewis is an assistant professor at Princeton University, Marc Tsurumaki is an adjunct professor at Columbia University, and David Lewis is an associate professor at Parsons The New School for Design.

Julieanna Preston's life as an academic, researcher and design practitioner spans architecture, landscape architecture, furniture design, construction, carpentry, interior design, urban design, and digital fabrication. Published internationally, she has most recently contributed towards advancing interior design with a book, *INTIMUS: Interior Design Theory Reader* (John Wiley & Sons, 2006), which she co-edited with Mark Taylor. She is internationally recognised as a champion of design as research through her creative and textual works on the architectural aesthetics of seismic strengthening (see *Moments of Resistance*, Archadia, 2000) and new urban furnishings derived from garment construction (see *Architectural Design Review*, RMIT, 2005, and *AD: Surface Consciousness*, Wiley, 2002). She works and lives in Wellington, New Zealand.

Charles Rice is a senior lecturer and MArch course director in the School of Architecture at the University of Technology, Sydney. He has also taught in histories and theories at the AA School of Architecture, London. He is author of *The Emergence of the Interior: Architecture, Modernity, Domesticity* (Routledge, 2007). His recent work is also published in the anthologies *Architecture and Authorship* (Black Dog, 2007), *Critical Architecture* (Routledge, 2007), *INTIMUS: Interior Design Theory Reader* (Wiley, 2006), *Negotiating Domesticity: Spatial Constructions of Gender in Modern Architecture* (Routledge, 2005) and *Walter Benjamin and History* (Continuum, 2005). He is also a member of the OCEAN design research network (www.ocean-designresearch.net).

The MIX House Team is a collaborative venture between **Joel Sanders**, **Karen Van Lengen** and **Ben Rubin**, and builds on their shared interests in architecture, technology and the human senses. Sanders is principal of Joel Sanders Architect (JSA) in New York City. A graduate of Columbia School of Architecture, his projects have been showcased in numerous international publications and exhibitions. He is an associate professor of architecture at Yale University. Van Lengen is principal of KVLA and Dean of the School of Architecture at the University of Virginia. A graduate of Columbia University School of Architecture, her award-winning design work has been widely published and exhibited. Ben Rubin is a media artist and founder of EAR Studio based in New York City.

Malte Wagenfeld is a practising designer who explorative designs have been internationally exhibited. Recent projects have focused on the design of experiential and perceptive environments rather than physical objects. His current design project, The Aesthetics of Air, at the Spatial Information Architecture Lab (SIAL) at RMIT, Melbourne, investigates the sensual and thermal possibilities of air movement within interior spaces. He is the Programme Director of Industrial Design at RMIT.

Lois Weinthal is a director of the Interior Design Program at Parsons The New School for Design. Her studio, Weinthal Works, focuses on the relationship between architecture, interior, clothing and objects, using questions and curiosities to inform design projects that take on an experimental nature. Grants include a Fulbright and DAAD Award with which she has developed design projects exhibited in Berlin and New York. She studied architecture at Rhode Island School of Design and Cranbrook Academy of Art.

CONTENTS

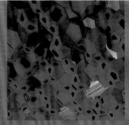

SANAA's New Museum of Contemporary Art, New York

When Kazuyo Sejima and Ryue Nishizawa, now of the Tokyo-based firm SANAA (Sejima and Nishizawa and Associates), were selected to design the New Museum of Contemporary Art in 2002, they seemed an interesting but strange choice, since the cutting-edge museum was moving to the Bowery, an area known more for its down-and-out residents than its art-world glamour. But, as **Jayne Merkel** explains, the architects have managed to produce a building that is both rough and ready and beyond the fray. It is already a rather mysterious landmark rising several double-height storeys above its gritty neighbours.

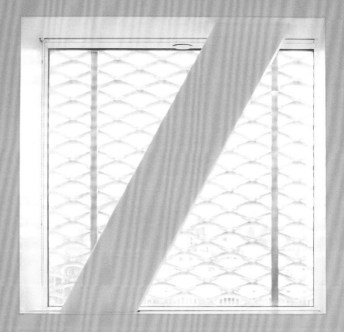

The Toby Devan Lewis Sky Room has 186 square metres (2,000 square feet) of glass-walled space for meetings and special events on the topmost occupied level of the museum. The flexible space is surrounded by an outdoor terrace on the east and south sides of the building, which offers views of classic New York water towers, midtown Manhattan to the north, the rough-and-tumble Lower East Side and bustling Wall Street on the south.

From half a mile away, the shimmering windowless boxes stacked slightly askew resemble the elegant, transparent SANAA buildings most New Yorkers know from pictures but not first-hand. Closer, the structure seems more solid, slightly porous and metallic until, from across the street, one can see that it is sheathed in an aluminium mesh skin. A 4.6-metre (15-foot) tall wall of windows faces the street. Another horizontal strip of glass cuts through the fourth floor where the Education Center is located. Otherwise the walls are opaque, covered with an elegant but industrial-strength aluminium screen in front of extruded aluminium panels. Mesh screening is also used to create a double-curved see-through wall inside on the entrance, enclosing the museum shop. A reception desk, cloakroom, café and long, narrow, skylighted gallery, also on the ground floor, are visible from the street and energised by views of the quirky scene outside.

The pristine, spacious, largely windowless galleries upstairs, however, are sealed vessels with few distractions, as they appear to be from a distance where they look like mysterious boxes. They cut the art off from the outside world, quite unlike Yoshio Taniguchi's elegant Museum of Modern Art (MoMA), which offers views of New York skyscrapers, the streets below, and other parts of the museum from many of its galleries. Instead of looking out on to the deprived neighbourhood nearby, those at the New Museum relate to it by the straightforward use of common materials.

The New Museum of Contemporary Art occupies an L-shaped site surrounded by restaurant supply stores, tenements, a flophouse and, one door away, the Bowery Mission, which serves the street people for whom the Bowery is famous. The Bowery is called Third Avenue a few hundred feet north where New York City's rigid rectangular street grid begins, but like most old streets in Lower Manhattan, it turns off at an angle. It is where winos and hoboes famously congregated during the Great Depression, and where their contemporary equivalents remain.

SANAA, The New Museum of Contemporary Art, New York, 2007
The wide-open unobstructed spaces in the New Museum galleries are supported by diagonal structural beams outside the building's boxes. These beams, painted white, are visible occasionally in windows like this one in the fifth-floor office area. Columns embedded in the elevator core also provide support.

The neighbourhood is changing fast though. It is only a few blocks east of SoHo where the New Museum was founded 30 years ago to show art more radical than that at the uptown museums. Its trustees decided to move away when the once-industrial neighbourhood stopped being the home of artists' lofts and galleries after the invasion of wealthy collectors and luxury shops in the 1990s. Now quirky boutiques line the streets of NoLita (for North of Little Italy), an area between SoHo and the Bowery that is clearly being gentrified, as the home of the New Museum may soon be. Though most of the established SoHo galleries moved to West Chelsea a decade ago, there are already 25, mostly smaller, art spaces near the museum already.

Physically, the new building will be fine if the area changes, because the design hovers curiously between industrial and elegant with silky polished concrete floors, plain white walls and white pipe railings. It is minimal and matter of fact at the same time.

'The Bowery was very gritty when we first visited it. We were a bit shocked, but we were also impressed that a contemporary art museum wanted to be there,' says Kazuyo Sejima. 'In the end, the Bowery and the New Museum have a lot in common. Both have a history of being very accepting, open, embracing of every idiosyncrasy in an unprejudiced

manner. When we learned about the history of the New Museum we were flabbergasted by its attitude, which is very political, fearless and tough. The New Museum is a combination of elegant and urban. We were determined to make a building that felt like that.'

The galleries, which fill the first, second and third floors, are the building's heart. They are all column free because support is provided by diagonal structural beams on the exterior coated with spray-on fireproofing and painted white, and by vertical beams in the concrete core that houses the elevators, stairwells and restrooms.

Bands of skylights along the west and north sides of the 5.5-metre (18-foot) tall, 465-square-metre (5,000-square-foot) first-floor gallery and on the east and west sides of the 6.4-metre (21-foot) tall, 372-square-metre (4,000-square-foot) second floor gallery reveal why the boxes are not piled directly on top of one another. Overhangs make it possible to bring in natural light from above, though most of the lighting is provided by fluorescent tubes suspended from striated metal panel ceilings, like those in warehouses only painted white. There are also a few old-fashioned mid-century modern canisters on lighting tracks. The sheetrock gallery walls are painted white, and the polished concrete floors are grey. The only glimpses of

The glass-walled entrance opens directly to a reception desk and elevators. The Museum Shop is off to the right, framed by a serpentine mesh screen. Behind it, a wide staircase leads to the underground theatre. The New Food Café at the rear of the space borders a 102-square-metre (1,100-square-foot) gallery behind a soaring glass wall illuminated by daylight filtering down from the shaft of the structural box above.

The first-floor galleries are the largest, but they have the lowest ceilings. Although there are skylights running for several feet along the west and north sides, where the box above steps back, most of the light is provided by fluorescent tubes set squarely on top of metal-panelled ceilings. Only careful placement and white paint makes them look different from those in a warehouse, but the polished concrete floors provide a certain elegance, albeit one familiar to commercial galleries but more carefully done here.

A series of stacked boxes contain the practically windowless galleries on the first, second and third floors, sealing them off from the raw Bowery neighbourhood, but recalling it with industrial materials. Setting each box several feet behind or beside the one below makes it possible to bring light into interior spaces with skylights. During the opening exhibition, the cool facade wore a neon rainbow lapel pin by the Swiss artist Ugo Rondinone that read, 'Hell, Yes!'

colour appear when the elevator doors open and their bright chartreuse walls appear – and, of course, in the art on display.

The art at the opening show, 'Unmonumental', was very raw – mostly free-standing montages made from old clothes, broken furniture and industrial objects jarringly combined. It seemed at home, but so would a roomful of elegant bronze sculptures or traditional oil paintings. The galleries are neutral, but not characterless. The 279-square-metre (3,000-square-foot) one on the third floor has an open metal staircase running along the north side, behind the elevator bank, with a little landing where a small work of art could be almost hidden. At the opening show, the work situated here was an 'Unmonumental Audio' (one of several throughout the galleries), so visitors could find it – and the little landing – fairly easily. But the tiny space would also accommodate a little treasure begging to be found only by the persistent. The third-floor gallery, though the smallest, is also the tallest, at 7.3 metres (24 feet). And it has southern skylights that wash it with natural light of various qualities at different times of the day and year.

The fourth-floor Education Center reconnects the institution to the neighbourhood with a big long band of windows, books about the Bowery, and computer terminals offering maps, views and interviews with artists who live – or lived – in the area. There are also videos and printed materials that tie the New Museum of Contemporary Art to similar institutions in other parts of the world.

The upper floors are off limits to the public except at weekends, which is too bad since the glass-walled meeting room on the sixth floor and the balconies around it offer some of the best views of New York anywhere. The

skyscrapers of the Wall Street financial district to the south seem almost within reach, as do the classic skyscrapers of midtown, a mile or so north.

Offices on the fifth floor are crisp, white, crowded and separated by striated translucent Polygal panels. They buzz with activity. The uninhabited tall seventh-floor box is open to the sky and contains mechanical services. And there is a 182-seat 'black box' theatre below ground which has white walls and an anteroom with a digital mural by Jeffrey Inanba plotting the global flow of political and cultural philanthropy.

The most intriguing thing about the New Museum is that, although its finishes are familiar, nowhere else are they used in quite this way. The anodised expanded aluminium mesh, which is manufactured in England, was originally used to stabilise roadbeds. Suspended over extruded aluminium panels and held in place by simple aluminium clips, it creates a single continuous surface of indeterminate depth. (The architects chose it because tests showed that the galvanised or stainless-steel panels that they had planned to use would soon become pitted in dirty New York air and the seams would show.)

The museum's proportions are unusual, as is the way each floor is set slightly in front of, behind, or off to the side of the one below. The building has an almost haunting presence on the skyline where it soars 53 metres (174 feet) above its neighbours, suggesting that something unusual is going on inside. The architects have done their job to tantalise potential visitors subtly. Now it is up to the curators to make it worth the effort for them to venture here again and again. ⚫+

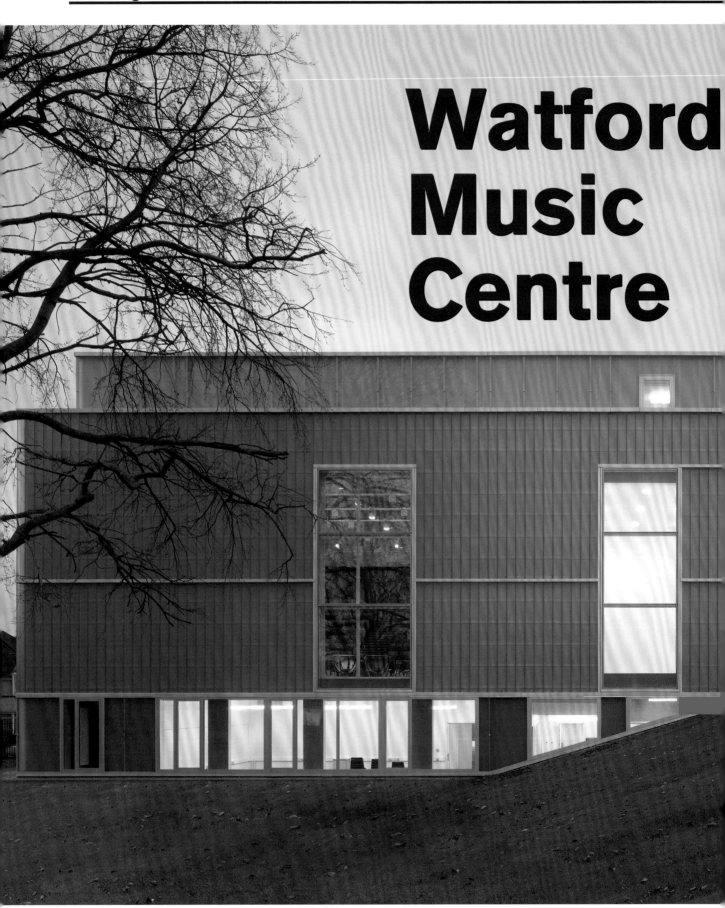

Watford
Music
Centre

David Littlefield describes how Tim Ronalds – the architect of the much-loved, restored Hackney Empire in London and the Landmark theatre in Ilfracombe, Devon – has, on a very tight budget, satisfied the ambitions of both the Watford Grammar School for Boys and the county council for a regional music centre.

By far the best place to talk to Tim Ronalds, architect of the Watford Music Centre in Hertfordshire, would have been the lofty recital hall – the primary performance space in this intelligently thought-out and well-made building. But the teenager beating out his own very personal rhythm on the drums showed no sign of stopping, and asking him to give it a rest would have been an act of the deepest irony. So we squirreled ourselves away in one of the many tuition rooms – compact, neat and wonderfully quiet.

Ronalds has done his profession a considerable service with this building, because the Watford Music Centre is proof (in an age when much proof is needed) that a skilled and clever architect can make all the difference to an inexperienced client with little money and naively big ambitions.

You've got a state-funded school with no funds at all, and a local authority, equally cash-strapped, with a big idea: to build a dedicated music centre for both pupils and the local community. Not any old music centre, you understand, but one with soundproofed rooms, recording and percussion studios, offices, tuition suites and an entrance/foyer worthy of a genuine civic building. It's a building where classes can swarm in and really own the place, like only schoolchildren can; but it is also a building where the middle class can enjoy a cultured night out.

Tim Ronalds Architects was selected from an RIBA shortlist and asked to steer the joint-venture client (the grammar school and the Watford School of Music) through the entire process. It was Ronalds who identified the spare bits of playing field that could be sold off for development; it was Ronalds who designed the housing to occupy those sites; it was Ronalds who negotiated a path through a complex, multiphase planning process; and it was Ronalds who concluded that siting a glass box right in front of the Grade II listed school building, dating from 1910, was a good idea.

Giving the music centre a high-visibility position adjacent to the busy Rickmansworth Road was, admits Ronalds, 'a rather surprising solution'. Keeping both clients happy and giving them an equal sense of ownership over the project was like 'keeping a marriage alive,' he says. In particular, the Hertfordshire County Council-funded Watford School of Music did not want its identity confused with that of the school, and hiding the new building around the back of the Edwardian-era main school would have been politically tricky. Indeed, the School of Music wanted its identity enhanced. The school itself, however, is maintained directly from Whitehall, rather than the county council, so a healthy dose of mutual suspicion accompanied the desire to jointly build and run this community facility.

When Ronalds first saw the site in 2001, the elegant main school was, in fact, already hidden from view by a wall of Leylandii. By cutting the trees down, Ronalds reasoned, the

Tim Ronalds Architects, Watford Music Centre, Watford, Hertfordshire, 2007
The music centre is a four-storey building that neatly straddles its sloping site. Although encased in glass, it is not a glowing box.

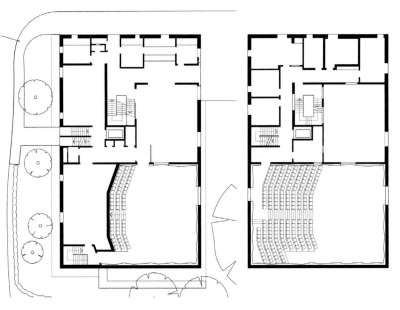

Ground-floor and first-floor plans. The drawings reveal how the space underneath the seats in the main performance hall is used as a greenroom – an assembly point for musicians.

The form of the Watford Music Centre is simple – it is a rectilinear form straddling the slope of the site, topped with a set-back upper storey that allows mechanical and electrical equipment to hide behind the parapet. Deliberately, this is not a building of solid and void, light and shadow: instead, it is an exercise in 'surface effects', achieved through the careful application of a glass skin.

'We wanted to make a building with a watery quality, something almost ethereal,' says Ronalds, who relishes the many tricks light plays on both the reflective float-glass windows and the more absorbent planks of Reglit glazing – staple-shaped strips of cast glass that are arranged back to back to form a double skin. He is right to be excited: even on the overcast, sodden day on which we toured the building, the Reglit managed to contrive a certain luminescence, even though it is backed by nothing more than cement board.

Inside, Ronalds has managed to make daylight work just as hard – an open, top-lit staircase (which threw up a number of fire regulations issues) brings light right into the heart of the building. Views both to the outside of the music centre and within it are very carefully framed; there is no window where there need not be one, and the size, shape and position of openings have obviously been the subject of a great deal of thought. The central foyer, which can double up as a sort of jazz café when required, is surrounded by vantage points that make this pivotal space seem bigger than it really is. You could stage *Romeo and Juliet* here.

This internal transparency is one of the things Ronalds is most pleased about. Another feature of the building that satisfies him is the circulation, which is almost never-ending. Because the music centre is built for performance, as well as tuition and rehearsal, the building contains many circuitous routes allowing musicians to enter a space from one side and depart on the other. You can virtually visit every room in this four-storey building without once retracing your steps,

school would gain a garden; furthermore, any objections that the new music centre would partially obscure the school building were countered by the fact that the trees had been doing that anyway.

Crucially, there was never any intention to replicate the form or materiality of the original school block. Ronalds was determined to steer through a contemporary building with its own distinct identity; rather than create a relationship between the new and old buildings, both buildings could each have their own relationship to the new lawn. It was a thesis that the local planning officer, who Ronalds describes as 'enlightened', was happy to entertain.

Clad in both highly reflective float glass and opaque Reglit, the facade of the music centre manages to become animated in all light conditions. The classical lines of the Neo-Georgian main school can be seen in the reflections.

The 200-seat recital hall is the music centre's principal performance space. The faceted walls and ceiling are part of the acoustic strategy devised with Arup.

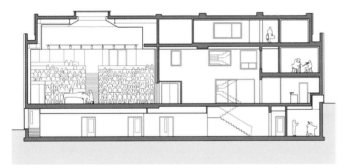

Long section through the building, illustrating how it negotiates the sloping site. The lower floor becomes a basement at its northern end.

making it flexible and porous enough to soak up large numbers of people effortlessly. On Saturday mornings hundreds of people can be milling about the place.

The original intention was to timber-clad the interior, but budget constraints forced a move to plasterboard, a cause of some disappointment for Ronalds. 'I fundamentally don't like plasterboard. I like things with more solidity,' he says. But he need not beat himself up over it, as this cheaper alternative works well – especially in the 200-seat recital hall where the faceted wall panels are accented by different shades of ochre. For such a large room it is a pared-back, gentle space that provides a relatively neutral backdrop to the vivacity of the performers. Not neutral in the 'white cube' sense; it is warmer than that. Many kids will perform here, and one would not want to scare the life out of them.

'The thing that mattered most was getting the feel of it right,' says Ronalds. 'When the kids come in, it shouldn't be overwhelming. There has to be a warmth and informality. You could have a space that's much more intimidating.'

What makes this building so good is that it could easily have become an exercise in robustness – physically and visually strong enough to withstand the knocks of heavy use. It is robust, of course, but it is also a place of some considerable finesse. And for £4.25 million, that is remarkable. ∆+

David Littlefield is an architectural writer. He has written and edited a number of books, including *Architectural Voices: Listening to Old Buildings*, published by Wiley (October 2007). He is also curating the exhibition 'Unseen Hands: 100 Years of Structural Engineering' which will run at the Victoria & Albert Museum from March to October 2008. He has taught at Chelsea College of Art & Design and the University of Bath.

Arup Associates

A specialist architectural division of the wider Arup group, Arup Associates has a unique composition and ethos. In its studios, teams of architects, structural engineers, environmental engineers, urban designers and product designers work alongside each other on the design of buildings from a project's inception. It is an interdisciplinary approach that the practice pioneered in the 1960s, and which has been reinvigorated in the last few years by a new emphasis on 'unified design' – a radical wholeness in thinking and execution. Here, **Jay Merrick** talks to Arup Associates' principal Declan O'Carroll and considers his vision of an architecture capable of addressing complexity and sustaining humanity in the face of modernity.

Vauxhall Transport Interchange, London, 2005

The pursuit of architecture in the 21st century puts its practitioners in vertiginous territory. Essential architectural reference points that once seemed usefully distinct – history, cultural norms, received notions of context and materiality – are today enmeshed in the increasingly influential gravities of the virtual. We have never known so little about so many things. The machines we live in are not buildings, but macro-economic constructs.

Our perceptions and sense of existence, our thoughts, emotions and actions, are subject to increasingly disparate asymmetries: Google, YouTube, MySpace, Facebook, Wikipedia; pathologically evasive ambiguity and irony; things that may be symbols, and symbols that may be things. Images, data and technology are only meaningful if they can be considered in wider, human relations; if they cannot, they seem mute and absurd. We are at risk of becoming supplicants to the iconic, and its Zen of architectural bling.

'Architecture is a human venture,' says Arup Associates director, Declan O'Carroll. 'We're looking at how to infuse a humble desire for the work to relate to people, and to carry an emotional resonance.' His comment lies in the shadow of increasingly brutal demographic, economic and cultural evidence. Mike Davis, author of *Planet of Slums*,[1] delivered a salutary drum roll of statistics in 2006, and here are some bullet points:

- by 2015, there will be 550 cities with at least one million inhabitants;
- by 2020, strip-cities will include a continuous 200-mile urban sprawl linking Accra in Ghana with the capital of Benin;
- one sixth of the world's population already exists in so-called 'informal sectors' whose anarchic entrepreneurial and housing modes are beyond the effective reach of statutory or monetary regulations.

The timing of Arup Associates' move into unified design, following successive iterations of the integrated design processes pioneered in the 1960s, reflects the increasing complexity of cities, and in particular their greater cultural diversity, their infrastructural and transport herniations, the remorseless demand for housing on sites of increasing difficulty, and the evolution of radically *laissez faire* education environments. These ingredients seem, at times, to be caught up in the slipstream of that most ubiquitous of displacement activities: consumption. And in this mall-like ambience, design processes are tainted by a mysterious matrix of velocities or inertias. The result is an expression of human erosion, or perhaps simple survival, rather than fertility.

'Many of the problems we witness in the world today are a result of design decisions,' says O'Carroll. 'This is not limited to the field of architecture. We are forming an over-indulgence on technology to solve our problems, many of which have been created by not recognising the impact of technology in the first place.'

Vauxhall Transport Interchange, London, 2005

The setting for the interchange would suit a modern-day Lear: the king's blasted heath replaced by the velocities and inertia of traffic, empty spaces and unremarkable existing buildings. Something momentous was required for this disjunctive urban site if travellers were not to feel like so many Beckettian Estragons and Pozzos waiting for the No 77 to Tooting.

Arup Associates' elegant steel-clad flight-path form brings a bold new elevational geometry to the area – a clarified signal of change and potential further regeneration in this dead spot behind the moderne haunches of the MI6 Building. The practice characterises the canopy as a ribbon, but it is a gestural post-Constructivist sculpture whose key features were prompted by the opinions of local people and stakeholders. It is significant that this relatively radical architectural presence was created after consultations right through the design phases. It was local demand that produced the *pissoirs* for homeward-bound clubbers, the open-sidedness, extended CCTV coverage and more retail points than originally mooted.

Drawing on their highly effective Plantation Lane project in the City of London, the practice added an artful security dynamic to the interchange by floodlighting it dramatically at night, making it a beacon rather than a shadowy realm. One result of this is that 40 per cent more buses now pass through it. The beacon effect is partly powered by the photovoltaic array in the upper surface of the final 'lift-off' section of the 200-square-metre (2,153-square-foot) canopy, whose angle maximises sun-strike in a way that might well have interested Malevitch.

Druk White Lotus School, Ladakh, northern Himalayas, due for completion 2011

The architecture of the Druk White Lotus School in northern India, generated by a unified design methodology, has retained the primacy of local formal and material traditions, but produced learning conditions that have drawn from more modern, transcultural experiences. The school, designed and built over a period of 15 years under the patronage of His Holiness the 14th Dalai Lama, draws 400 pupils to the village of Shey in the Himalayas, to a new model for education founded on both current local needs and potential cultural development.

The whole-life sustainability pursued here is about more than reducing energy consumption. The essential design issue was how human culture – tradition, religion, the intangible components of humanity – might be sustained in the face of modernity. Arup Associates' design touchstone was the prioritisation of individual experience, values and local identity through a design that would thoroughly engage the senses and memory.

The design process was collaborative, allowing free voice to local advocates of certain aspects of the project – an integration of inputs, free of inappropriate influence by an externally imposed architectural vision. The construction of the school relied on local materials, labour and tools, so virtually all the detailing was traditional. Thus the Druk White Lotus School is not an architectural anomaly; the school buildings' formal clarity and firmness bring only a carefully considered hint of western architectural commodity to this faraway place.

BSkyB Transmission and Recording Facility, Hounslow, London, due for completion 2010

Two very different paradigms for communications architecture are on the way. Rem Koolhaas and Arup's CCTV Building, under construction in Beijing, will be the first grand architectural icon of the 21st century, based on scale and formal virtuosity. The other paradigm will be Arup Associates' massive Harlequin 1 Building at BSkyB's Osterley campus, near Hounslow. Its architectural significance lies in the way unified design has pursued extreme functional efficiency, maximisation of social spaces, and what is expected to be the world's most environmentally sustainable broadcasting and data centre.

The 100 x 50 metres (328 x 164 feet) building, whose mass is equivalent to two New York blocks, will house recording, post-production and transmission facilities. The architecture of the building was developed in tough consultations with dozens of Sky stakeholders, and personally encouraged at key moments of innovation by James Murdoch, head of European and Asian operations. The result, among other things, is the world's first matrix of large, naturally ventilated recording studios.

This is 21st-century power station architecture whose 13 super-scale vent stacks, two elegantly twisted windmill towers and biomass plant signal its impendingly vast output of digital and graphic communications energy. The design passed through 10 iterations, with subpathways, as the architects reasoned against initial demands for a high-tech box that served technology rather than overall working conditions.

Two key innovations arose from the fusion of architectural risk and ambition implicit in Arup Associates' unified design approach. Originally, the building's reception volumes were mute: one would enter a neutral space, get in a lift, and then become hermetically sealed in a functional zone. The final design has, instead, created a series of light-filled reception and break-out volumes at various levels, emphasising human presence and nonprofessional activity.

The other breakthrough feature is the naturally ventilated studio complex. Here, air movement is prompted by waste heat rising from studio lighting-rigs. Hot air is expelled upwards through enormous exhaust stacks, drawing in fresh, cool air through a sound-attenuation plenum just below the slightly raised ground-floor slabs. For a substantial portion of the year, no extra energy will be needed to pull the air through the studios.

O'Carroll believes that 'our era is image-dominated like no other. This has been reinforced through technological invasion allowing us to produce what Italo Calvino has described as an unending rainfall of images. The dominance of vision is apparent everywhere. The manifestation of the image, and the ever-developing modes of transmission, are saturating us. Our experience of space and time has become diffused and confused. The visual image has become an experience commodity. Our other senses are becoming desensitised.'

Progressive, inclusive debate about design processes is under threat. The profession risks losing any sense of an interdependent usefully volatile condition of enquiry from which new modes of design response can evolve; a common place of ideas, reactions and actions, as it were, inhabited by humane motives, and by certain highly sensitive relations of expertise capable of expressing and communicating those motives.

'Architecture requires us constantly to reinterpret and revalue technology in human and social terms,' wrote Arup Associates Philip Dowson in a 1980 publication, *Contemporary Architects*. His conviction was that 'close-knit, interdisciplinary design teams were necessary to confront the scale and complexity of modern buildings if an architecture is to survive which embodies humane ideas ... However, whilst method and analysis can never substitute for an architecture which helps to enrich and not diminish our lives and surroundings, nevertheless, in considering means and ends, the ends have become so complex that it has become necessary to design new ways of designing new buildings, if an architecture is to be derived from all the sources that can nourish it.'[2]

Dowson's views had been even more directly expressed by Hugo Häring. As Colin St John Wilson noted, Häring disconnected himself from the prefigured Rationalism of Le Corbusier's Five Points in 1925 by declaring a search for architecture that discovered its own forms.[3] Four years later, Eileen Gray warned that technology was hermetic: the means of building was becoming more important than the purpose, which was joy and and self-fulfilment.[4]

In these resonant ideas we see that Arup Associates' 21st-century quest to establish a unified design ethos – a self-levelling compass in the widening phenomenological gyre, as it were – retains the genetic markers for practice set out 27 years ago by Dowson. Today we might query certain dynamics in Sir Philip's remarks, notably his implication that, in the face of increasing architectural complexity, the way to reduce inhumane effects is to apply cross-fertilised intelligence to projects capable of 'creating an environment for mass need'. There is a tension between this Modernist instinct to design for mass need (with its peculiar suggestion of a singular entity) and the idea that the way to do it is to absorb 'all the sources that can nourish it'. That tension remains, quite properly, in the practice's current ambitions for unified design. But Dowson's credo has developed into a language of engagement and interpretation based on individual rather than mass need. O'Carroll's metaphors and references not only reflect our phenomena-saturated times; they are field-maximising tools that establish a mindset of inclusion, more effective tessellations of individual responses, and the allowance of unpredictable design possibilities.

Thus unified design will tap more sources: various kinds of artists, social scientists, cultural commentators – anyone who can enrich design at an early stage, make it more responsive and humanely ambitious before form and programme are defined. The human, physical experience of buildings is seen

'Our approach to design is one that attempts to sustain all the components of humanity, and concerns itself with sustaining individual lives in a holistic way'

as crucial. 'Our approach to design is one that attempts to sustain all the components of humanity, and concerns itself with sustaining individual lives in a holistic way,' says O'Carroll. 'We're not talking simply about reducing energy consumption. We believe the real issue is how human culture – tradition, religion, joy, pain and the intangible components of humanity – can be sustained in the face of modernity. There's a need to reprioritise the importance of the details of human experience by communicating and enriching the physical, the sensual, the imaginative and the contextual.'

In considering Arup Associates' new direction, it is interesting to look back at the firm's earlier projects of the 1970s and 1980s. One finds a powerful diagrammatic and elevational clarity, and relatively restrained formal or material brutality. The practice's architecture in that period was both innovative (Harold Wilson's 'white heat of technology' still echoed) and artistic, in a measured way. The mediating human touch was found in the detail. Consider the understated elegance of the slim arcade columns and shallow arches below the Vaughan Building at Somerville College, Oxford, the vertically striated bricks at Ampleforth College, the concrete handrail mounts at the CEGB regional headquarters near Bristol, or the engrossing mixed materiality of the entrance at Leckhampton House at Corpus Christi, Oxford.

'The domain of architecture is unique among the arts,' says O'Carroll. 'It carries a greater burden of direct responsibility. Unlike the traditional domains of other arts, where the relationship of engagement is by choice and consent, architecture is by its nature omniscient. It can be unforgiving in its impact on people. Our modes of creation should be cognisant of this responsibility. No other art has the ability to directly enhance the quality of people's lives; and no other has the capacity to inflict as much misery.

'Our built environment is inextricably linked to our sense of self. It acts as a key influence in the quality of our whole-life experience. As a backdrop to support diversity of experience it is entirely natural that this manifests itself in an array of different and often contradictory ways. This *bricolage* of

environments is in harmony with the diversity that feeds our whole-life experience. This complexity contrasts with the key influences directing many contemporary architectural creative methodologies, which are overly simplistic in comparison.

'Our engagement with architecture is dependent on the senses; it is only through the senses that architecture comes to life and exerts its full potential. Our senses integrate our experience of the world. Our architecture needs to rediscover its potential to stimulate all the senses.'

Arup Associates is pursuing the opposite of a unified language of architecture. O'Carroll notes that 'if you take a complex form, reflect it in a mirror, and then smash the mirror, you only see part of the whole in a shard. In a hologram, a shard reveals the whole image, the whole complexity. What we're interested in, through unified design, is not the Miesian idea of the god in the detail. Part of our desire is a level of honesty in the way we articulate this message.'

The practice's quest for engaging, humane architecture requires design processes that may be based on unfamiliar scenarios; on ideas and research drawn, as O'Carroll puts it, from a kind of peripheral vision where unexpected contextual or interpretive possibilities are noticed: 'We have to be inventive enough to capture the speed of change.' Arup's research unit is now, as a matter of course, using interactive designer–client spatialisation and visualisation software, and programmes designed to reveal unexpected information about organisations that could usefully inform conceptual reactions and refined design. The research unit also spends time assessing the crossover potential of innovations in non-architectural fields. More is more.

'If elements of experimentation and research cannot exist outside of their own reality,' says O'Carroll, 'then their overall contribution is limited, and compromised. The focus of the next generation of pan-disciplinary collaborative partnerships will be in generating new creative techniques and methods in order to unify the whole. Unified design develops a method of creativity that is more than the sum of individual disciplines. Instead, the boundaries are blurred, and the very process of design maximises the potential of collective creativity.'

Jay Merrick is architecture critic of *the Independent*, London, and has written on architecture and art for publications including *Blueprint*, *New Statesman*, *Architects Journal*, *ArtReview* and *Art and Auction*. His novel, *Horse Latitudes*, was published by Fourth Estate in 2000.

Jay Merrick's essay 'Unified Design: A Radical Wholeness' on the work of Arup Associates is featured in *Unified Design: Arup Associates*, edited by Paul Brislin, published in April 2008 by John Wiley & Sons, ISBN: 978-0-470-72331-9.

Notes
1. Mike Davis, *Planet of Slums*, Verso Books, 2007.
2. Philip Dowson, in Ann Lee Morgan and Colin Naylor (eds), *Contemporary Architects*, St James Press (Chicago and London), 2nd edn, 1987, p 243.
3. Colin St John Wilson, *The Other Tradition of Modern Architecture*, Black Dog Publishing, 2007, p 32.
4. Eileen Gray and Jean Badovici, 'From Eclecticism to Doubt, *L'Architecture Vivante*, Editions Albert Morancé, Autumn 1929, p 20.

Can Architectural Design Be Research?

So far the Unit Factor series has focused on design research within the context of the Architectural Association in London. Here the series editor, **Michael Weinstock**, discusses the possibilities of architects undertaking research in practice. He draws on the experience of Chris Bosse, who is responsible for the competition-winning design for the Watercube, Beijing's National Swimming Centre.

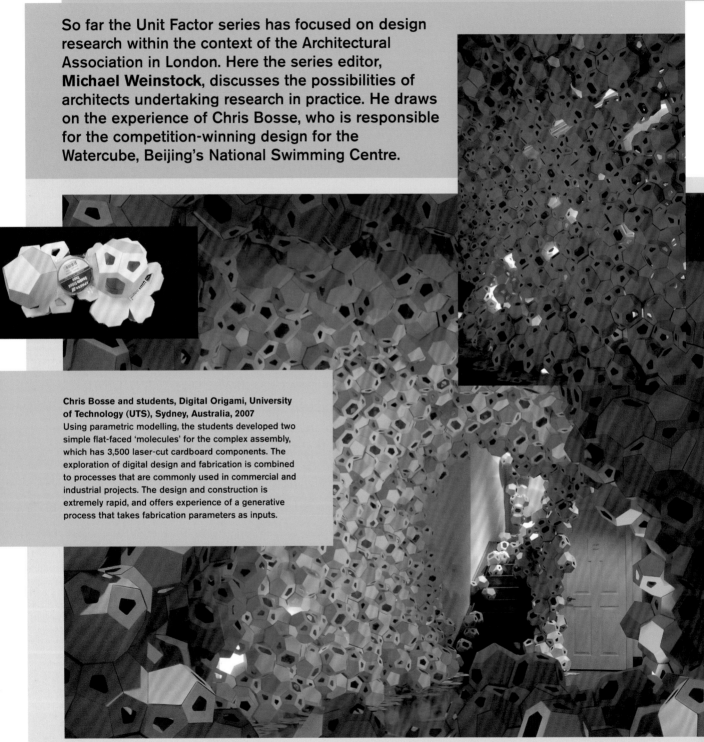

Chris Bosse and students, Digital Origami, University of Technology (UTS), Sydney, Australia, 2007
Using parametric modelling, the students developed two simple flat-faced 'molecules' for the complex assembly, which has 3,500 laser-cut cardboard components. The exploration of digital design and fabrication is combined to processes that are commonly used in commercial and industrial projects. The design and construction is extremely rapid, and offers experience of a generative process that takes fabrication parameters as inputs.

Is there really such a thing as 'design research' in architecture, and if there is why is it not more widely accepted by the world at large? Many architects will agree with the argument that each design is in answer to a set of questions and circumstances that are unique, and so every design is 'research'. On the other hand, it is also commonly accepted that that every design project takes place within the context of a widespread and quite uniform set of material systems, industries and construction processes. And it is clear that the practice of architecture, in the profession and in academia, is conducted very differently to the aircraft, automobile and consumer product design industries. In these industries, research is organised as a well-funded specialist activity, and new designs can undergo prolonged experimentation, testing and refinement before going into production. Architectural designs often have to achieve an optimal resolution of conflicting parameters without extensive testing, and must be constructed under strict time, financial and material constraints. Experimentation is fine as long as it does not cost any more than existing methods, or take any longer. So is it possible for an architect to really do design research?

In the sciences, research is usually defined as an inquiry, conducted through a close and careful study, that is intended to yield new knowledge, or integrate existing knowledge in a new synthesis. Hypotheses are proposed, and experiments are designed to test them, and either the hypothesis is proven, or if not the hypothesis is modified. So far so good – a new and untested design is evidently a hypothesis, and constructing a design is the ultimate test. It might be thought that the significant difference between the processes of scientific research and design research lies in the repeatability of experiments, and in the full disclosure of data and methodology. Architects, and indeed other designers, do not habitually share such details – but the material context in which architectural designs are realised is so widespread that the only part of the whole process that is not openly available is the generative act of design. If the general ambition of research is to be new, and the general ambition of design is

Chris Bosse, Entry Paradise Pavilion, Zeche Zollverein, Essen, Germany, 2006
The form of the membrane was produced through an iterative series of simulations, including a space-packing algorithm that subdivides the whole volume. The spatial model was then developed as a continuous minimal surface, and optimised for the cutting pattern using sail-making software. The 500 cubic metres (17,657 cubic feet) of membrane weighs only 17 kilograms (37.5 pounds), and can be put up or taken down in one hour.

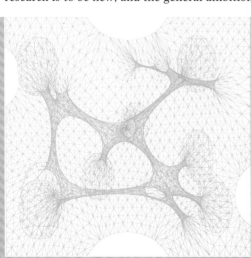

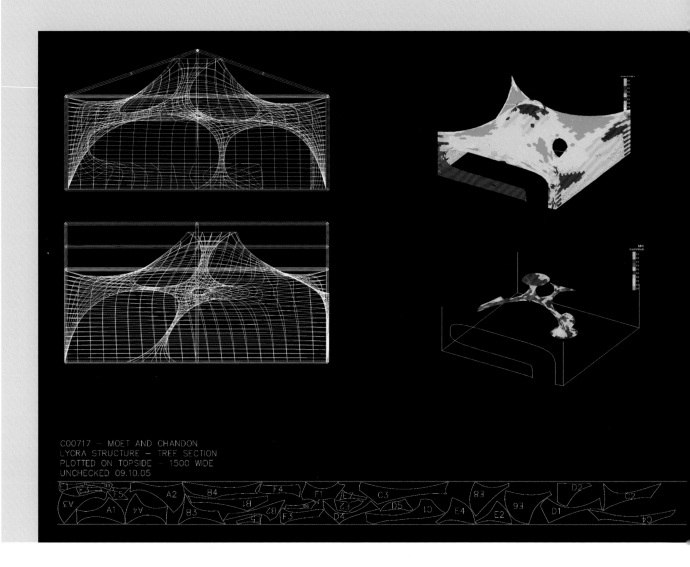

C00717 — MOET AND CHANDON
LYCRA STRUCTURE — TREF SECTION
PLOTTED ON TOPSIDE — 1500 WIDE
UNCHECKED 09.10.05

to be optimal, then design converges with research when the design goes beyond existing forms, or spaces, or material systems, and is realised in the general context of architectural production. Architectural research is possible, but tends to proceed by incremental advances, and longer term research goals have to be conducted through a series of realised experiments.

Finding or creating opportunities for 'design research', and simultaneously developing a professional practice has been the ambition of many young architects over the last century or more. The 'atelier' tradition has been reformulated in the contemporary world, and the pursuit of new forms, spaces and material knowledge can be most often be seen in small and temporary constructions. Chris Bosse exemplifies many of the characteristics of the new generation of 'atelier' architects – he was educated in Germany and Switzerland, and produced the competition-winning design for the Watercube, Beijing's National Swimming Centre, while working in Australia with PTW Architects and their partners in China. Currently nearing completion, the Watercube has been widely acclaimed as a unique and innovative design.

Bosse has recently set up his own office, the Laboratory for Visionary Architecture (LAVA), in Sydney, working, with his partner Tobias Wallisser, who is based at LAVA Stuttgart, on series of high-end international projects in conjunction with PNYG in the Middle East and elsewhere.

Bosse is also a presence on the international lecture circu His research interests lie in the development of unconventional forms that are constructed from single material systems that simultaneously produce structure and define space. The design method arises from the computational simulation of the growth and morphologies c natural systems, and the abstraction from those systems of rationalised systems of repetitive but varied elements. The studies of bubbles and foam that led to the design and construction of the Watercube are now well known, but perhaps less well known are the small projects that Bosse ha designed and constructed.

Three recent small projects exemplify the continuity of experimentation, using methods related to the Watercube, and tested in constructed pavilions.

The Moët Marquee/Espace lumiere for the Melbourne Cup

Chris Bosse and Amanda Henderson (Gloss Creative), Moët Marquee/Espace lumiere, Melbourne Cup, Australia, 2005
The digitally developed form was constructed from translucent Lycra, and weighs 35 kilograms (77.2 pounds). The strong daylight is filtered from above by a metal screen, and the fabric is also patterned, so that the natural changes in daylight during the course of the day produce varied light conditions within the space. The cutting pattern for the fabric runs concurrently with the optimisation process, so that iterations of form automatically produce the optimal pattern.

Australia's largest horse-racing event, in 2005 was designed and constructed with Amanda Henderson of Gloss Creative, occupying a 10-metre (32.8-foot) cube of space with a membrane structure of a total weight of only 35 kilograms (77.2 pounds). The perforated ceiling above directs sunlight on to the translucent Taiyo–Lycra fabric, the changes in natural light during the course of the day giving a dynamic and ephemeral quality to the space.

The following year Bosse produced the Entry Paradise Pavilion for the Zeche Zollverein design exhibition in Essen, Germany. The pavilion was designed and constructed in just four weeks. It is a membrane structure that is clearly descended from, but different to, its ancestor, and fills a 7-metre (23-foot) cube of a dark interior without the use of conventional methods of dividing and separating. The programmable lighting emphasises the taut minimal surface curvatures of the nylon stretching between floor and ceiling. The structure defined the entry space of the exhibition, and the total weight of only 17 kilograms (37.5 pounds) means that the whole thing can be packed into a sports bag and transported and reused elsewhere. As with the Moët Marquee, construction time is one hour.

Both designs emerge from the computational process, and the meshed surfaces of the digital model directly generate the cutting pattern for the membrane. The operative parameters of sail-making software and digitally controlled cutting machines are inputs to the growth of the computational model, so that design and production are integrated in the design process from its initiation.

The Digital Origami installation (2007) was designed and constructed by students of the University of Technology (UTS), Sydney, where Bosse is an innovation fellow. The space-filling structure is created from only two variant forms of cardboard components. The mathematical concept stems from the same space-packing algorithm explored in the Watercube structure, but using surface forms rather than nodes and struts. The aim of the generative process was to test the idea, common in natural forms, that a very small set of components can be used to construct very large and complex forms.

We tend to think of research as a lonely occupation conducted in a laboratory or library. However, research in any field is conducted with other people, and this is particularly the case with design research. While not every architectural design project can truly be said to be research, the work of Chris Bosse confirms that design research is possible for architects even while they are in practice. It can be pursued in constructed designs that extend existing ways of making forms and spaces, and in the development of innovative material systems. The pursuit of larger ambitions and grander research goals may be advanced by finding opportunities in more numerous small and ephemeral projects. The development of a research agenda in the context of a continuing series of small constructed projects is an evolutionary strategy appropriate to both architect and client. The architect stands to gain knowledge and expertise, and the client stands to gain an innovative design that is built on a previous success.

In the next article a different mode of design research and practice will be explored in an account of the work of the multidisciplinary practice Design to Production.

Unit Factor is edited by Michael Weinstock, who is Academic Head and Master of Technical Studies at the Architectural Association School of Architecture in London. He is co-guest-editor with Michael Hensel and Achim Menges of the *Emergence: Morphogenetic Design Strategies* (May 2004) and *Techniques and Technologies in Morphogenetic Design* (March 2006) issues of *Architectural Design*. He is currently writing a book on the architecture of emergence for John Wiley & Sons Ltd.

SPILLER's BITS

Architects as Hairdressers

Neil Spiller reactionary? Spiller finds himself recoiling into a 'grumpy old man' as he observes the emergence of an alarming new trend in architecture schools that prioritises style over matter.

It is often said: 'It's a wonderful time to be an architect.' Certainly in London, architects are insulated from the 'credit crunch' by the work generated by the 2012 Olympics and Crossrail. Architectural students are also more numerous now than they have ever been. On a more international and cultural level, our profession is now opening up to the many different ways in which architects may practise. Space is seen as a synthesis between the virtual and the actual. Even cosmological space is beginning to be thought of as architectural (with all its problems – I certainly do not want to see the Golden Arches superimposed on my view of the Moon!). Technology, while fraught with ethical dilemmas, is providing infinite architectural possibilities. We have also seen beyond the silly dogmas of Modernism and are starting to develop more meaningful architectures (well, a few of us are!). Well this all sounds great: 'Oh how lucky we are to be architects aren't we?' Alas NO!

I am fortunate, if you will excuse the expression, to 'get about a bit', and old enough to remember how things have been in the last 30 years. I've been to many, many architectural schools and in a brief synopsis these are my recent observations. There is often a denial of new technologies and subsequently new conceptions of space. Old mythologies of pedagogy are prevalent (the benefit of the studio as a learning device, for example). Outdated notions of multidisciplinarity are often lauded, being confined to the usual building consultants. This is all par for the course, depressing though it is. But a new, much more dangerous affectation is rearing its pretty head in some of the most forward-thinking architecture schools. I shall call it the 'Architect as Stylemeister'. In many ways the architects of the next generation are now seeing themselves as a kind of architectural hairdresser: no content, just style.

Ian Laurence and Karl Normanton, Pie Shop, Bloomsbury, London, 2005
This drawing shows the differing elements of the scheme and their integration.

The project seeks to integrate itself with its surroundings and feeds off the peculiar mix of adjacent urban uses which includes a dance studio.

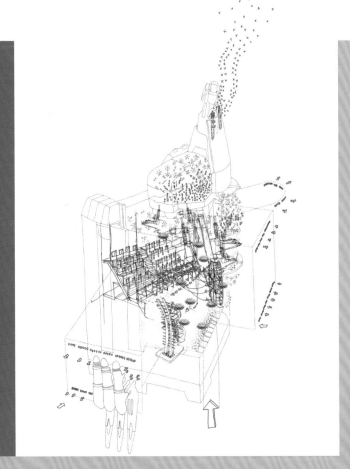

The influence of the dance studio permeates into the pie shop, and a theatrical pie-serving and eating regime is developed.

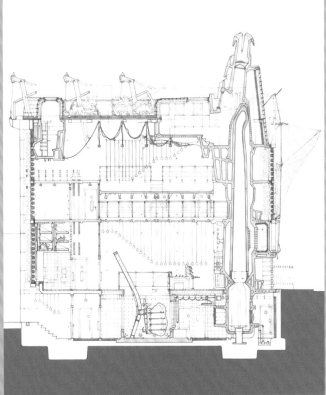

Section showing the level of innovation in the scheme generally.

For the first time, in my ever lengthening career, I have been made to feel reactionary and it is a feeling I do not like. I was recently at a big international show crit. Critics had flown in from around the world. The work on the wall was gorgeously presented. Many Chinese labourers' yearly wages had been blown on printing the renders that in themselves had taxed some of the finest turbocharged computers. And so the critting commenced: no plans, no useful sections, no idea of structure, no integration of environmental concerns, no synthesis of the functions on the inside and the overall forms on the outside. Normally, when these issues are brought to a student's attention, after a brief and often sophist defence they acquiesce. But here a certain pride manifested itself. 'It is someone else's job,' I was told on numerous occasions. Which is this new profession that does everything that architects used to do except styling? And what happens to a profession that gives up its ability to synthesise many priorities and scales of operation to achieve a beautiful whole? I'll tell you what happens: no one takes it seriously. It loses its power – and no power, no work.

In the UK, I often hear colleagues bitch about the Architects Registration Board demanding that each graduating student can show a reasonable and proficient knowledge of how a medium-sized building can be designed in all its aspects – technical and ecological. You will not hear any such silliness from me. That is the easy bit of architectural education and should be accepted as given. The hard bit of educating architects is giving them the mental dexterity with which to cope with the massive ontological changes that will occur in the nature of architecture over the next few decades.

I am illustrating this 'Spiller's Bits' with an example of what I consider a good attempt by two, then fourth-year, Bartlett architectural students, Ian Laurence and Karl Normanton, to be innovative with structure, programme, construction, multivalence, materiality, environment and context. This was merely one term's work, and beats mere highfalutin styling that would fall down, kill babies and leak, any day.

An analogy with pornography might be useful. Porn is fine, but sometimes you want to have a relationship. And as with the stylemeisters, the objects of porn are often exploited. Before all you normative architects out there shout 'Rejoice, Spiller's come over to our side,' forget it. I will be back for you later. △+

Professor Neil Spiller is Professor of Architecture and Digital Theory and Vice Dean at the Bartlett, University College London.

Biofuel from Algae

Finding an alternative fuel for our built environment as a substitute for fossil fuels is the Holy Grail of a sustainable future. **Ken Yeang** discusses the potential of mass algae production as a source of biofuel. Could we be powering our buildings and cars with algae in years to come?

We have already gone past the halfway point in our consumption of all the available fossil oil fuels on earth. Gasoline will become increasing costly, and it is predicted that within the next 20 years governments will insist that unless a building can generate its own energy, it will not receive development approval – a step that will radically change our approach to architectural design.

Could algae fuel, as a third-generation biofuel, be the solution? A low-cost, high-yield biofuel, it gives out 30 times more energy per square metre than any other biofuel crop.

The harvesting of algaculture for producing vegetable oil, biodiesel, bioethanol, biogasoline, biomethanol, biobutanol and other biofuels is also becoming increasingly commercially viable. Its main advantage is that algae can also grow on marginal lands, such as in desert areas where the ground water is saline, and recent advancements have also shown that they can grow vertically on a light armature.

Predictions from small-scale production experiments indicate that using algae to produce biodiesel may provide enough fuel to replace current world gasoline usage.

The use of biofuels in place of fossil fuels and natural gas is reliant on the efficient production of liquid and gas biofuels using cheap organic matter, agricultural and sewage waste that yield high net energy gain. Another advantage of many biofuels over most other fuel types is that they are biodegradable, and hence ecologically acceptable.

Predictions from small-scale production experiments indicate that using algae to produce biodiesel may provide enough fuel to replace current world gasoline usage. However, the solution for the future of urban transportation needs to be totally rethought and reinvented rather than maintaining the status quo of a car-based urban economy.

Micro-algae also have much faster growth rates than terrestrial crops. The per-unit area yield of oil from algae is estimated to be from between 4.6 and 18.4 litres per square metre (5,000 and 20,000 gallons per acre) per year – a yield up to 30 times greater than the next best crop. After algae and oil palm, the Chinese tallow (*Triadica sebifera*) is the third most productive vegetable-oil bearing seed crop in the world.

The difficulties in the efficient production of algae biofuel lie in finding an algal strain with a high lipid content and fast growth rate that is simple to harvest, and in creating a cost-effective cultivation system (for example, a type of photobioreactor – see below) best suited to that particular strain. Another obstacle has been the type of equipment and substructure needed to enable mass algae growth.

The conventional open-pond system of growing makes the entire effort dependent on the hardiness of the strain chosen, requiring it to be unnecessarily resilient in order to withstand wide swings in temperature and pH, and competition from invasive algae and bacteria. Open monoculture systems are also vulnerable to viral infection. However, one approach is to grow the algae in thin-walled polyethylene tubing called Algae Biotape, which is similar to conventional drip irrigation tubing and can be incorporated within a normal agricultural environment.

An algal strain with a high oil content is generally less hardy or has a slower growth rate. Algal species with a lower oil content, not having to divert their energies away from growth, can grow more easily in the harsher conditions of an open system.

Though in a closed system, where the algae are not exposed to the open air, there is no risk of contamination by other organisms, the problem is finding a cheap source of the sterile carbon dioxide (CO_2) required for this type of system. Sources could be industrial smokestacks or even conventional power plants, which would also help soak up the pollution. Thus algae production in combination with existing coal-power plants or sewage treatment facilities, for example, not only provides the raw materials required for the system; it also completes the ecological cycle by changing the wastes into resources.

Recent experiments in the field of algal cultivation have used marine micro-algae in a photobioreactor – a bioreactor that incorporates some form of light source. Almost any

Vertigro Energy, a joint venture between Global Green Solutions and Valcent Products, is a technology for the mass production of algae by a bioreactor that grows the algae vertically for extraction of the algae oil. The oil is cost-effectively refined into a nonpolluting diesel biofuel. The algae-derived fuel is an energy-efficient, environmentally friendly replacement for fossil fuels and can be used in any diesel-powered vehicle or machinery.

translucent container can be a photobioreactor; however, the term is commonly used to define a closed system of production. An enclosed pond (for example covered by a greenhouse) is another form of photobioreactor.

Photobioreactors can be operated in 'batch mode'. However, the introduction of a continuous stream of sterilised water containing nutrients, air and CO_2 is also possible, though this results in a higher-maintenance system. As the algae grow, excess culture overflows and is harvested. Continuous bioreactors such as this fail very quickly if they go unmonitored, but under the right conditions they can continue operating for long periods. An advantage of this type of culture is that algae produced in the 'log phase' generally have a higher nutrient content than old senescent algae. Maximum bioreactor productivity occurs when the exchange rate (time to exchange one volume of liquid) is equal to the doubling time (in mass or volume) of the algae.

Two substantially different closed photobioreactors have recently been developed: the tubular photobioreactor (made of rigid or collapsible tubes) and a vertical alveolar panel (VAP) made of 1.6-centimetre (0.6-inch) thick Plexiglas alveolar sheets. The advantages of the vertical tubular reactors are their high surface-to-volume ratios, smaller ground footprint, low shear forces, low cost, absence of wall growth, CO_2 usage efficiency, and their ability to optimise the use of natural sunlight.

The next stage for architects is the integration of these photobioreactors with building design. Perhaps the skyscraper of the future will have a series of integrated photobioreactors on its south-facing facade, connected to a biomass energy-generation plant.

Ken Yeang is a director of Llewelyn Davies Yeang in London and TR Hamzah & Yeang, its sister company, in Kuala Lumpur, Malaysia. He is the author of many articles and books on sustainable design, including *Ecodesign: A Manual for Ecological Design* (Wiley-Academy 2006).

McLean's Nuggets

Self-Organisation and Environmental Improvisation

Two recent talks, one by an architect and one by an educationist, both referenced the Game of Life and its self-organising properties which, through a simple rule-based approach, can model seemingly complex systems.

The mathematician John Horton Conway devised the Game of Life in the late 1960s based on an earlier proposition by John Von Neumann for a universal computer. The Game of Life is the most widely known form of cellular automata.[1] The rules are simple. On a Cartesian grid (of infinite size), a number of cells are placed with the 'rule-base' stating that the proximity of its eight adjacent cells (diagonals are included) will determine the state of their neighbours, with cells living or dying depending on how many surround them. Cells can die of overcrowding or loneliness, and can come alive if surrounded by the correct number of living adjacencies. However, it is only through the rapid iterations of this digital Petri dish that patterns become visible, including 'gliders' whose life cycles create a continuous physical movement across a grid, and cell groupings that exist in dynamic equilibrium (geographically stationary, but in a continually oscillating state).

Architect Pete Silver, in a talk entitled 'Machine intelligence and postwar housing',[2] described his work in the early 1990s as a research associate in the Land Use Research Unit at King's College London under Professor Alice Coleman. The research sought to correlate the design of postwar planned housing with long-term environmental and social breakdown, and resulted in a £50 million Department of the Environment grant to redesign some of the most run-down housing estates in Britain. The talk was given against the background of Silver's long-term interest in the use of the computer as a modelling tool. During the talk, Silver showed extracts of the extraordinary Land Use maps produced at the time and the complex statistical data-gathering methods used. Central to Coleman's project was a set of design remediation tools with which tenants could exercise self-determination (organisation) and ownership of their own 'defensible space'.[3]

Meanwhile, Sugata Mitra[4] (Professor of Education Technology, Newcastle University) speaking at a PAL[5] Lab event in Kent suggested that school without teachers and without a physical base might be the best bit of self-organised learning that we could possibly have. His Hole In The Wall projects developed in India seek to explore how children learn collectively, self-regulate and self-organise. By providing public access (for children only) to the Internet in remote Indian villages he has sought to study how these untutored and uncoerced children learn to navigate the World Wide Web despite language and cultural differences. This also led to Professor Mitra's observation that children are overburdened by an almost impossible number of rules designed to govern what they should and should not do. Self-organisation and determination may be enabled by a set of designed circumstances, but the parameters of these circumstances, if too restrictive or various, will prevent any natural (or unspecified) growth.

Artist Dave Carr-Smith,[6] speaking at a debate on the future role of architecture, asked: 'How can potential individual (and small collective) environmental improvisations be incorporated in the planning process?', his proposition being that 'Functionally-unspecialised public environments are necessarily more enriched by "citizens initiatives" than by "official" or designated planners'. If our architectural palette is limited, then we should invent or appropriate new ways and means and stop being unnecessarily curtailed by a collective failure of imagination and enjoy the inventive potential and the fruits of individual and group self-organisation.

Pete Silver, Mozart Estate, Exploded volumetric showing principal subdivisions, Design Improvement Controlled Experiment (DICE) project, Land Use Research Unit, King's College London, 1994.

Computational fluid dynamics (CFD) model of airflow and air quality within an office.

Glassless Society

Before we hide ourselves completely behind the triple-glazed, argon-filled, neoprene-gasketed, ultra-reflective noncrystalline amorphous solid (also known as glass), it might be worth revisiting JD Bernal's *The Social Function of Science*.[7] In chapter XIV, 'Science in the Service of Man', Bernal describes a French locomotive (steam at the time) where the grot-prone glass in the locomotive's front windows were replaced with 'baffle-guarded' clear openings. Never mind self-cleaning glass; what about no glass at all? Has our technological ingenuity really been stretched in the development of the ephemeral climatic enclosure? Bernal continues: 'Considerable developments may be expected in the application to buildings of aerodynamic principles, the least of which would be the abolition of draughts.' So how about a more creative application of the increasingly ubiquitous tools of computational fluid dynamics (CFD), to analyse these 'aerodynamic principles', and design surface morphologies with which to ventilate and protect internal climate by designing and envisioning airflows and turbulence? While we are at it, dispensing with hitherto acceptable architectural devices, why not dump the door, or at least the ones that we have to manually push, pull or slide? Retailers clearly understand the benefit of a 'barrier-free' threshold, utilising the not exactly new invention of the automatic door opener/closer or the more lightweight solution of an air curtain. Yes there may indeed be running costs, but think of all the embodied energy saved.

Magic Architecture

The case for Magic Architecture and indeed Magic Engineering is one worth constantly restating. In 1936, architectural magician Frederick Kiesler stated that: 'Magic Architecture is the expression of the creativeness of man ... it is not dream architecture ... it is the architecture of everyday, every-night reality.' Kiesler, the diminutive genius and creator of the Universal Theatre and Endless House, continues: 'It [magic architecture] performs wonders in the development of mankind, just like sunlight performs wonders in the development of plants, being a constant environmental companion.'[8]

More recently, structural engineer Chris Wise declared: 'We have more than enough engineers. We need magical conjurors.'[9] That is to say that in response to critic Jonathan Glancey's call for 'an army, navy and air force of engineers'[10] to sort out the UK's infrastructural problems, Wise says 'we need better engineers ... more thinkers', adding that: 'Nowadays, sums are so easy that many engineers try to analyse their way to an answer, diligently solving the wrong problem, rather than think their way to a solution.'[11] △+

'McLean's Nuggets' is an ongoing technical series inspired by Will McLean and Samantha Hardingham's enthusiasm for back issues of *AD*, as explicitly explored in Hardingham's *AD* issue *The 1970s is Here and Now* (March/April 2005).

Will McLean is joint coordinator of technical studies (with Peter Silver) in the Department of Architecture at the University of Westminster.

Notes
1. JH Frazer, *An Evolutionary Architecture*, Architectural Association (London), 1995.
2. University of Westminster School of Architecture and the Built Environment, Technical Studies evening lecture, 15 November 2007.
3. O Newman, *Defensible Space: Crime Prevention Through Urban Design*, Macmillan (New York), 1972.
4. www.ncl.ac.uk/ecls/staff/profile/sugata.mitra
5. www.pallabs.org/
6. http://www.davecarrsmith.co.uk/
7. JD Bernal, *The Social Function of Science*, George Routledge & Sons (London), 1939.
8. FJ Kiesler, *Selected Writings*, Verlag Gerd Hatje (Germany), 1996.
9. C Wise, 'Response', *Guardian*, 14 November 2007.
10. J Glancey, *Guardian*, 15 October 2007.
11. C Wise, op cit.

Space on Earth

A Virtual Portal Between the Earth and Outer Space

Whereas those such as Richard Branson are pioneering tourist travel into outer space, **Valentina Croci** investigates a project that will allow visitors to take a virtual trip into space. She describes how, in an unknown city location, the interdisciplinary international practice F.A.B.R.I.CATORS is running an ambitious project that will provide a space simulation close to earth.

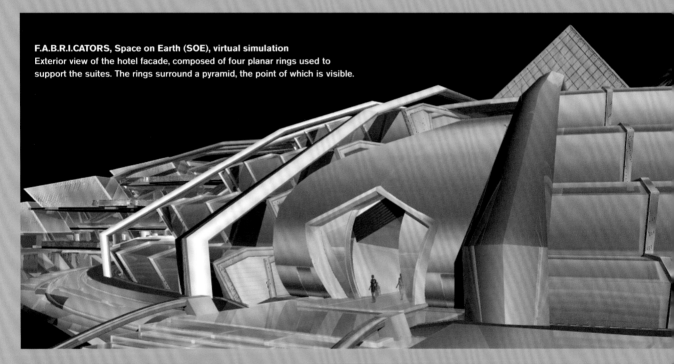

F.A.B.R.I.CATORS, Space on Earth (SOE), virtual simulation
Exterior view of the hotel facade, composed of four planar rings used to support the suites. The rings surround a pyramid, the point of which is visible.

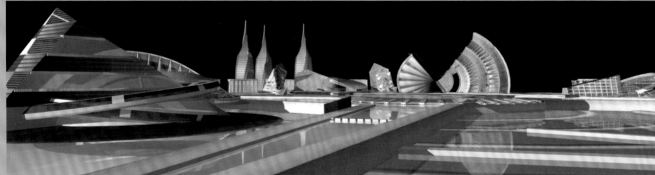

Master plan for SOE with eight buildings and a ring of real estate. In addition to two hotels, one of which is the SpaceGate Hotel, there is a theme park with a theatre, the transportation hub and the educational research centre. The last is intended to host two university departments, a computer graphics study centre and a centre to study life in SOE. The project may also include a satellite station connected with other spatial research centres and, finally, the 'brain' for the management of online gaming and interaction inside SOE.

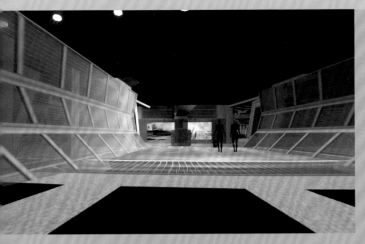

Interior view of one of the bridges that connect the rings, beyond   which it is possible to see into the SOE city.

The shuttle station inside the SpaceGate Hotel.

The conquest of outer space remains a part of our collective imagination. Who is not fascinated by the idea of navigating galaxies and visiting the planets of the solar system? This common dream lies at the base of Space on Earth (SOE), a city for the virtual navigation of outer space, due to be constructed in an area that measures one kilometre (0.6 miles) in diameter (the exact location is yet to be revealed). SOE is both a physical and a metaphorical portal: it is a city based on the economic organisation, services and infrastructures of a 'real' urban context that allows visitors to take a virtual trip into space, together with other users.

This large project is being run by F.A.B.R.I.CATORS, an interdisciplinary group founded in Milan in 1990 to pursue the integration between new media, communication and the classical arts, primarily through virtual-reality projects. The office is composed of five founding members from different backgrounds, including Franz Fischnaller, an artist, expert in digital media and professor at, among other institutions, the Electronic Visualisation Lab (EVL) at the University of Illinois, and Yesi Maharaj Singh, a journalist with a degree in curatorship, museology and art administration from New York University. The office itself features approximately 30 staff, located in different offices around the globe, and can count on a vast network of business and academic partners and professional consultants.

The SOE master plan is a freeze-frame of the Milky Way, covered by eight structures: two hotels, one of which is known as the SpaceGate Hotel, a theme park and theatre, an educational research centre and an urban traffic hub, all of which are surrounded by a ring of real estate. Given the complexity of the project, SOE will be completed in phases. To date, the city has been developed as a virtual-reality simulation. The first viewing of the project took place at the VIEW Conference held in Turin in November 2007, while the first simulation of the SpaceGate Hotel is being presented as part of the retrospective dedicated to the work of Franz Fischnaller at the Museo Archeologico Virtuale (MAV) at

Interior view of the foyer at the ground floor, with a glimpse of the satellites that float overhead. The design of the spaces in virtual reality requires an extreme level of attention in the reality of the images (lighting, reflections and shadows, proportions, changes in perspective and so on). The user is immersed in images from various directions that change simultaneously at 360° at his or her discretion.

Herculaneum, Naples. As part of the development of this first virtual phase (due for completion in 2008), plans call for the creation of immersive environments with multiple screens to simulate the presence of users in the Space City and during the navigation of the galaxy. Users can interact on- and off-line in real time using immersive platforms located at other sites around the globe.

The second phase of the project corresponds with the physical construction of the SpaceGate Hotel, and later, in several phases, the construction of the other SOE buildings (the project schedule, financial partners and developers for this have not yet been revealed). SOE will be a sort of Shangri-La that will, however, actually exist thanks to real money and real investments, allowing for its overall sustainability.

The interior of the SpaceGate Hotel, a physical structure whose floor plan measures 140 metres (459 feet) in diameter, will feature a simulation of the SOE and the spatial

View of the interior of the bridge that connects the four rings, showing the solar panels that provide energy for the structure. The continuous vision between the various levels of the hotel and the uninterrupted perception of cosmic space are impressive.

View of the interior of the upper ramp at the topmost level, with the bridges that connect to the various levels and the exterior structures for the landing the space shuttles. The image of the hotel is similar to that of a spaceship.

navigation of the universe. The project for the hotel shows four rings that wrap around a pyramid of the same dimensions in scale to the Cheops pyramid. The structure contains 300 suites, and ramps and hallways that provide access to common areas for entertainment and services. The physical construction of the SpaceGate Hotel will allow for a convergence of the virtual, and augmented and mixed reality. Virtual reality will be created using digital avatars that allow for interaction with other users of the city and the online community in the rest of the world. The interior of the hotel will be an augmented space, where the real and the virtual merge on the threshold of space. High-resolution displays and autostereoscopic visualisation systems are located in the halls and corridors, allowing visitors to feel as if they are in outer space.

Tracking systems allow visitors to interact with the computer-generated environment and communicate with its avatars, and intelligent built-in sound systems increase the field of perception. The interior of the SpaceGate Hotel will be a mixed-reality experience: halfway between the real and the simulated world, between the normal activities of humankind, such as the sharing of space and the inhabitation of a community with its rules, and access to virtual functions in some cases remote.

The ambitious SOE project and, in more general terms, the versatility of virtual-reality technology, induces a revision of the concept of architectural morphology: we are no longer dealing only with fixed, physical environments, but with supports structures in which the 'skin' of architecture changes according to the level of interaction between man and technology. The user experiences the environment that he or she chooses to see. In analogous terms, in these environments located somewhere between the physical and the virtual, there is an overlapping of that which users perceive of real architecture and what takes place on screen. Physical construction must thus be capable of favouring the

The immersive, stereoscopic screen environment in which the user wears 3-D glasses. The subject can interact with his or her avatar, or move through virtual environments using the rectangular-screen interface. It shows operable functions and changes in the Cartesian position of the user with respect to the MetaNet Page (MNP) that he or she observes.

experience of simulation – this is the case with the SpaceGate Hotel, where physical geometries must enhance the loss of Cartesian orientation, a characteristic of spatial navigation.

SOE is not simply a project for entertainment, but an extreme experiment of cohabitation with technology and an attempt to extend, to the maximum limits, the possibility of connection, even social, offered by the same technologies. It raises a number of issues, at the sociological level, of the evolution of the architectural and engineering professions, and the applicative limits of digital technologies, often meeting with heavy criticism. Notwithstanding this, however, the SOE project is not without its interest, and is equally curious due to its utopian nature and the basic idea of not rendering technology a simple and self-referential media.

Translated from the Italian version into English by Paul David Blackmore

Valentina Croci is a freelance journalist of industrial design and architecture. She graduated from Venice University of Architecture (IUAV), and attained an MSc in architectural history from the Bartlett School of Architecture, London. She achieved a PhD in industrial design sciences at the IUAV with a theoretical thesis on wearable digital technologies.

Virtual simulation of spatial navigation using avatars.

Exterior view of the upper bridge connections.

Permeating Walls

Howard Watson describes how Bennetts Associates' design to redevelop the Royal Shakespeare Theatre at Stratford-upon-Avon offers not only the opportunity to reconnect with the Warwickshire town, but also to interact with both the local community and the theatre's audience.

Bennetts Associates, Royal Shakespeare Theatre, Stratford-upon-Avon, Warwickshire, 2007–10
Aerial cutaway visualisation of the new theatre, viewed from the Bancroft Gardens side.
Charcoalblue, a specialist theatre-design consultancy, is collaborating with Bennetts Associates on aspects of the design, including the auditorium.

Permeability is essential to theatre. The Holy Grail is the connection, a level of interaction, inclusiveness and exchange between the live performance and the audience, which carries a unique charge that cannot be replicated. Yet unwelcoming theatre architecture, both interior and exterior, has done its best to ensure that the art form is often subject to claims of impermeability, elitism and even of cultural apartheid, and the Royal Shakespeare Theatre (RST) in Stratford has long given credence to the charge. Michael Boyd, artistic director of the Royal Shakespeare Company (RSC), has a vision of connectivity, of tearing down the walls. The challenge he set Bennetts Associates was to appear to do this while actually leaving many of those walls intact.

Bennetts is a 90-strong practice with offices in London and Edinburgh, and has received RIBA awards for the new-build Hampstead Theatre, London, and Jubilee Library, Brighton. On the £112.8 million RST project, architect Simon Erridge says that one of the challenges 'was to work within the existing structure and unify all the elements; the other was to make the institution of the RSC more approachable'. The RSC must connect with its wider locale, not just because of funding, but because its relationship with Stratford, Shakespeare's birthplace, is necessarily symbiotic.

Sitting alongside the Swan Theatre, a 1980s thrust stage conversion by Michael Reardon of the burnt-out Victorian theatre, the Grade II listed Royal Shakespeare Theatre, designed by Elisabeth Scott in 1932 in a rather functional style, and a series of later additions made the building even more foreboding and unapproachable. The facade along Waterside, the road that faces the town, was so inexpressive of the artistic intent within that it was known as 'the Jam Factory'. Inside, the building was cramped to the point of being unworkable, and the proscenium-style stage made connection with the audience difficult. This relationship will be utterly changed by the introduction of a new auditorium featuring a thrust stage, so that theatre-goers are grouped closely around the action, rather than feeling so remote.

The RSC's relationship with the outside world, Stratford and its townspeople will be painstakingly redefined. The success of Bennetts' design has been to translate Boyd's intentions into an invasion of topical lines of connection: new threads lead from the town to the theatre and through the theatre buildings themselves. This has been achieved while raising the profile of the best elements of the original building and making good use of its river- and park-side location.

A tower will announce the new orientation of the RST's relationship with its surroundings, becoming a notable feature of the skyline while also acting as a viewing platform for the town. Erridge says that Boyd wanted a 'flypaper, signalling the building for a new audience', and he hopes that it provides a beacon for the RSC's vision of inclusiveness. In fact, 'beacon' seems an

The Courtyard, a temporary theatre designed by Ian Ritchie, was built so that productions could continue during the construction period. The auditorium serves as a working prototype for the RST.

appropriate word as the design brings to mind a Japanese-influenced lighthouse. The body is made up of red brick, with the thickness of the piers narrowing as they rise to give a tapering effect, and it is graced by a glass lantern with louvres that will be open in summertime. The design is influenced by the geometrical qualities of the existing building, including its most notable Art Deco treasure, the foyer's marble staircase, designed by John C Shepherd. The tower marks the new entrance on Waterside and also provides vertical circulation.

The Waterside facade itself will be transformed. The new Theatre Square precedes the glass-and-steel entrance, which will lead into a glass colonnade that runs the length of the RST and along to the Swan. Thereby, the idea of the public piazza will extend through the outer wall, breaking down the division between town and theatre. The colonnade opens into a new, covered foyer area which will be shared by the RST and the Swan, aiding orientation and accessibility. The public will be able to go straight through the entire new building, both from the street to the river terrace and from the gardens on either side.

The Bancroft Gardens facade has been retained, but it is now adorned by a floating roof, and Scott's design re-emerges with a graceful symmetry. The riverside facade has been cleared so that there is a newly accessible river walk from the public gardens, alongside the theatre and onwards to the Church of the Holy Trinity, Shakespeare's burial place. Under the floating roof, a new restaurant will make full use of views over the Avon. For each new element, permeability is the key. Threads of public life, topicality and history have been spun throughout the scheme, invading the formerly off-putting, castle-like facades to create a new web of associations and connections.

Howard Watson is an author, journalist and editor based in London. He is co-author, with Eleanor Curtis, of the new 2nd edition of *Fashion Retail* (Wiley-Academy, 2007), £34.99. See www.wiley.com. Previous books include *The Design Mix: Bars, Cocktails and Style* (2006), and *Hotel Revolution: 21st-Century Hotel Design* (2005), both also published by Wiley-Academy.

Visualisations showing the new Theatre Square and glass entrance, and the view of the restored Bancroft Gardens facade, augmented by the new floating roof and tower.

Subscribe Now

As an influential and prestigious architectural publication, *Architectural Design* has an almost unrivalled reputation worldwide. Published bimonthly, it successfully combines the currency and topicality of a newsstand journal with the editorial rigour and design qualities of a book. Consistently at the forefront of cultural thought and design since the 1960s, it has time and again proved provocative and inspirational – inspiring theoretical, creative and technological advances. Prominent in the 1980s and 1990s for the part it played in Postmodernism and then in Deconstruction, in the 2000s ⌀ has leveraged a depth and level of scrutiny not currently offered elsewhere in the design press. Topics pursued question the outcomes of technical innovations as well as the far-reaching social, cultural and environmental challenges that present themselves today in a period of increasing global uncertainty. ⌀

SUBSCRIPTION RATES 2008
Institutional Rate (Print only or Online only): UK£180/US$335
Institutional Rate (Combined Print and Online): UK£198/US$369
Personal Rate (Print only): UK£110/US$170
Discount Student* Rate (Print only): UK£70/US$110

*Proof of studentship will be required when placing an order. Prices reflect rates for a 2007 subscription and are subject to change without notice.

TO SUBSCRIBE
Phone your credit card order:
+44 (0)1243 843 828

Fax your credit card order to:
+44 (0)1243 770 432

Email your credit card order to:
cs-journals@wiley.co.uk

Post your credit card or cheque order to:
John Wiley & Sons Ltd.
Journals Administration Department
1 Oldlands Way
Bognor Regis
West Sussex PO22 9SA
UK

Please include your postal delivery address with your order.

All ⌀ volumes are available individually. To place an order please write to:
John Wiley & Sons Ltd
Customer Services
1 Oldlands Way
Bognor Regis
West Sussex PO22 9SA

Please quote the ISBN number of the issue(s) you are ordering.

⌀ is available to purchase on both a subscription basis and as individual volumes

○ I wish to subscribe to ⌀ *Architectural Design* at the **Institutional rate of (Print only or Online only** *[delete as applicable]***)** UK£180/US$335

○ I wish to subscribe to ⌀ *Architectural Design* at the **Institutional rate of (Combined Print and Online) UK£198/US$369**

○ I wish to subscribe to ⌀ *Architectural Design* at the **Personal rate of UK£110/US$170**

○ I wish to subscribe to ⌀ *Architectural Design* at the **Student rate of UK£70/US$110**
⌀ *Architectural Design* is available to individuals on either a calendar year or rolling annual basis; Institutional subscriptions are only available on a calendar year basis. Tick this box if you would like your Personal or Student subscription on a rolling annual basis.

Payment enclosed by Cheque/Money order/Drafts.

Value/Currency £/US$ ☐

○ Please charge £/US$ ☐ to my credit card.
Account number:

☐☐☐☐☐☐☐☐☐☐☐☐☐☐☐☐☐☐

Expiry date:

☐☐☐☐☐☐

Card: Visa/Amex/Mastercard/Eurocard *(delete as applicable)*

Cardholder's signature ☐

Cardholder's name ☐

Address ☐
☐
☐ Post/Zip Code ☐

Recipient's name ☐

Address ☐
☐
☐ Post/Zip Code ☐

I would like to buy the following issues at £22.99/US$45 each:

○ ⌀ 193 *Interior Atmospheres*, Julieanna Preston

○ ⌀ 192 *Versatility and Vicissitude: Performance in Morpho-Ecological Design*, Michael Hensel + Achim Menges

○ ⌀ 191 *Cities of Dispersal*, Rafi Segal + Els Verbakel

○ ⌀ 190 *Made in India*, Kazi K Ashraf

○ ⌀ 189 *Rationalist Traces*, Andrew Peckham, Charles Rattray + Torsten Schmiedekneć

○ ⌀ 188 *4dsocial: Interactive Design Environments*, Lucy Bullivant

○ ⌀ 187 *Italy: A New Architectural Landscape*, Luigi Prestinenza Puglisi

○ ⌀ 186 *Landscape Architecture: Site/Non-Site*, Michael Spens

○ ⌀ 185 *Elegance*, Ali Rahim + Hina Jamelle

○ ⌀ 184 *Architextiles*, Mark Garcia

○ ⌀ 183 *Collective Intelligence in Design*, Christopher Hight + Chris Perry

○ ⌀ 182 *Programming Cultures: Art and Architecture in the Age of Software*, Mike Silve

○ ⌀ 181 *The New Europe*, Valentina Croci

○ ⌀ 180 *Techniques and Technologies in Morphogenetic Design*, Michael Hensel, Achim Menges + Michael Weinstock

○ ⌀ 179 *Manmade Modular Megastructures*, Ian Abley + Jonathan Schwinge

○ ⌀ 178 *Sensing the 21st-Century City*, Brian McGrath + Grahame Shane

○ ⌀ 177 *The New Mix*, Sara Caples and Everardo Jefferson

○ ⌀ 176 *Design Through Making*, Bob Sheil

○ ⌀ 175 *Food + The City*, Karen A Franck

○ ⌀ 174 *The 1970s Is Here and Now*, Samantha Hardingham

○ ⌀ 173 *4dspace: Interactive Architecture*, Lucy Bullivant

○ ⌀ 172 *Islam + Architecture*, Sabiha Foster

○ ⌀ 171 *Back To School*, Michael Chadwick

○ ⌀ 170 *The Challenge of Suburbia*, Ilka + Andreas Ruby

○ ⌀ 169 *Emergence*, Michael Hensel, Achim Menges + Michael Weinstock

○ ⌀ 168 *Extreme Sites*, Deborah Gans + Claire Weisz

○ ⌀ 167 *Property Development*, David Sokol

○ ⌀ 166 *Club Culture*, Eleanor Curtis